Appreciations for *Co*

From Couples and Individuals

"This is a fantastic guide to a healthy relationship. It will undoubtedly help many couples. Congratulations and get it out into the world!" Glenn and Elisabeth

"This book is a great tool for really identifying what it takes to sustain a relationship. It's written in a manner that allows for deep self-reflection, and it clearly outlines the steps that are needed to achieve a vital relationship. The goals are realistic, transparent, and thoroughly explained, making it easy to recognize the strengths and areas that need to be addressed to optimize and improve a relationship." D. F.

"I like the use of Respect, Trust, Unity, and the other Character Qualities as guides to reflection for the couples. A gift to the community and the world." Johanna Merritt Wu

"*Couple Vitality* is an information-packed toolkit with a wealth of ideas and techniques that a couple can use as they need to deepen their relationship. With a wide range of topics including discovering shared values, establishing a friendship, communicating about money, and many more, a couple can focus on areas they need to strengthen, or they can go through the book more systematically. I found the suggested exercises to be clear, helpful, and thought-provoking. I plan to return to this book many times as a valuable resource for communication about important topics and to improve my relationship." Anne Bivans

From Professional Colleagues

"This book is thorough, incredibly positive, and full of examples and strategies—exactly what couples need. I especially like the idea of a relationship as one of the best places to work on character and the book's clear theme of building character. (I am reminded of one of my favorite Frank Pittman lines, "marriage is your last best chance to grow up!".) I applaud you for what is obviously a deep dive into the research to provide such a practical, positive guide for couples to truly create a vital relationship. I am confident this information will help oh so many people." Pat Love, EdD; patlove.com

"This book is the answer to many couples' prayers. Some are clearly in the dark looking for a way out of the madness called their marriage or their relationship. They desperately want *Couple Vitality*. This book gives them exactly that and so much more. If you want a better relationship and want to put your heart into making that happen, start reading tonight. Dreams do come true." Nisa Muhammad, DMin; weddedblissinc.com; founder of Black Marriage Day

"This book isn't for couples who want quick-fix tips or who are recreational dabblers into having a good relationship. It's for couples who are all in and understand how their relationship is the foundation for changing the world—for couples who want nothing less than complete transformation. Kudos to the authors for their in-depth yet approachable concepts." Priscilla Hunt, Executive Director, Better Marriages; bettermarriages.org; closecompanions.org

"I like the content of the book. I find the tie-in to Character Qualities intriguing, and I like that it is character-based and not faith-based." Paul Kuhn, serving couples with his wife through their church and Better Marriages for 25 years

Couple Vitality

Connecting with Character

Susanne M. Alexander and
W. Grant Peirce IV

Couple Vitality

ISBN: 978-1-940062-29-7

Publisher: CharacterYAQ
(DBA of Marriage Transformation LLC)
Printer: IngramSpark®, United States of America

Contact Information:
www.characteryaq.com; www.marriagetransformation.com
susanne@marriagetransformation.com; +1.423.599.0153

Cover Design and Model Graphic: Steiner Graphics
Cover Photographer: Kanstantsin Markevich
Layout: Marriage Transformation, LLC

Couple Vitality

Table of Contents

Welcome!

Creating a couple relationship can be the most wonderful and the most challenging experience you both undertake in your lives. It has highs, lows, and moments when you are stuck in problems. Maintaining a relationship is a dynamic process of growth, and you will need to persevere with consistent effort over time. You can do it, and we are here to guide you.

As character and relationship professionals, we bring together for you some of the most important insights from science, stories from couples, personal experiences, and our own professional observations. We integrate the most powerful and dynamic aspect of your interactions that connect you as a couple: your characters. We will share with you how to use Character Qualities as a new "language" of connection between you.

What is Couple Vitality?

Vitality means that your couple relationship is alive, growing, and energizing for both of you. You appreciate being together, and the flow of energy between you is strong and positive. You can accomplish many aspects of life together that would be more difficult as individuals. There is a powerful unity and connection between you. Couple vitality strengthens as you consistently apply the Core Elements and Vitalizers in this book.

> "... [I]t is only in the context of connection with others that our deepest needs can be met. Whether we like it or not, each of us has an unshakable dependence on others. ... We need camaraderie, affection, love. These are not options in life, or sentimental trimmings; they are part of our species' survival kit. We *need* to belong."[1] Les and Leslie Parrott

Healthy couples make and keep a commitment to be together. Couple vitality builds when two healthy individuals strive to be excellent partners to one another. They consciously act in relationship-enhancing ways from the beginning of their connection. They also choose to apply Character Qualities to move their words and actions in a positive direction toward each other. They strive each day for new levels of growth and connection.

Vitality, Character, and Becoming "Us"

This guide is full of science-based tools and information to assist you with improving the quality of your relationship. As a couple, you will be full of vitality—the power to live and grow. The earlier you learn and apply character-based habits, behavior patterns, and ways of interacting, the happier and more vibrant your relationship will be. You will be less likely to inflict damaging wounds on each other.

Every couple is unique, and you will develop your view of what couple vitality looks and feels like for you. Below is one person's view.

> "[Couples] ...have an intimate connection. They make joint decisions about life, talk about things before decisions are made, communicate love and respect to each other on a daily basis, and are able to talk about anything without fear of judgment, put-downs, or criticism. They have an intimate emotional connection. They could be away from each other for weeks due to work and come back and pick up a conversation right where they left off. They have a healthy and satisfying sex life. Their time together is as comfortable as their feet in a favorite pair of slippers on a cold winter night. They curl up in each other's arms, knowing they are loved, cared for, respected, appreciated,

and listened to. Words don't even need to be exchanged all the time, because both husband and wife understand each other."[2] Kevin Leman

Does this describe "couple vitality" to you? Or would you want to create something different? Here are some of the key concepts in this guide to accompany you with creating your couple vitality:

- Two individuals come together and commit to creating a unified and interdependent partnership, which is a third entity, more than the sum of the two individuals. It includes their stories, histories, experiences, and creative outcomes (such as children!), all of which stand together and cannot be separated.

- The two individuals become unified as they become part of something larger and integrate their individual needs with their partnership. They use words like "we", "us", and "ours" instead of "I", "me", and "mine".

- Each partner has character strengths and growth areas that dynamically affect the quality of a couple's interactions.

- As a couple reflects, consults, and interacts in character-based ways, they build their unity and develop shared values and a vision for their relationship.

- Through developing and integrating Character Qualities with specific actions, a couple creates vitality in their relationship.

- They both strengthen the Character Quality of Unity, which empowers them to contribute to one another, their couple vitality, and to others.

- A couple continually reflects, consults, interacts, builds connection, and increases commitment, all of which create vitality.

- As they encourage each other and grow as a couple, they use Character Quality of Creativity to celebrate together. Throughout their relationship-building process, the partners develop their characters and increase their connection and vitality.

Note: There are 22 Character Qualities focused on in *Couple Vitality*. These 22 are listed below and defined in "Core Element C: Character Growth". You might have noticed that "Creativity" and "Unity" were capitalized above. Throughout the book, when the 22 Character Qualities appear, they are Capitalized to draw your attention to them and to differentiate them from other uses of the words.

1. Adherence
2. Compassion
3. Creativity
4. Dependability
5. Excellence
6. Flexibility
7. Friendliness
8. Honor
9. Humility
10. Justice
11. Moderation
12. Orderliness
13. Perseverance
14. Positive Spirit
15. Purposefulness
16. Reflection
17. Respect
18. Self-Discipline
19. Service
20. Trust
21. Truthfulness
22. Unity

These Character Qualities are derived from the Character Foundations Assessment™, a validated instrument developed by author W. Grant Peirce IV. Taking this assessment may assist you in understanding your orientation toward each Character Quality and subsequently with implementing the content of this book. You can contact either of the authors to take the assessment and receive an accompanying insights session with either of them or with another certified practitioner. See "About the Authors and Our Contact Information" at the end of the book.

Customize Your Approach

It's best if you take the content of this guide, pay close attention to the principles and their application, and then customize your approach to create the couple relationship full of vitality that works for the two of you. Some suggestions are provided in the next section. You may also seek other sources of information or spend time working with a professional.

In this guide, we illuminate the path to healthy relationships and shine a light on the importance of including character-based words and actions at all stages in your journey. We have seen the benefit with our own marriage partners and also in our clients' relationships, and we are confident that this is the way to a better future for you.

Welcome to *Couple Vitality*!

Susanne M. Alexander and W. Grant Peirce IV

Suggestions for How to Use This Guide

Determining Your Approach

Using this guide will be interesting, fun, and challenging. It will empower you to build a practical toolkit with information, ideas, and techniques that you can use as you need. This guide is like a blueprint, and you are the builders of your relationship. It's likely wise to start with one simple goal and gradually add in more as you build strengths.

Each chapter includes a key concept, and you will determine together how much time to spend on each one. You may already be skilled at the focus of a particular chapter and choose to spend your time on other ones. Your lives are probably full of many activities, so making a regular date with each other to discuss this material and carry out activities will keep it a high priority.

You may discover it's difficult to study together or you have limited time available. If so, you may delegate or take turns with one of you doing the study and sharing key points with the other. Then discuss the section together. If one of you is unlikely to read the book, the other might read it and apply the learning, which in turn will help the other see their positive example and appreciate practicing it themselves.

As needed, please take a break for relaxation, social time, and conversation. Your efforts at times may feel intense, but the goal is to bring you together in connection and to maintain your well-being throughout.

Step 1, Section 1: Powerfully Creating Vitality

The book begins with chapters that introduce you to three Core Elements under the heading of "Section 1: Powerfully Creating Vitality". These are listed below.

1. Unity
2. Reflection and Consultation
3. Character

These three are foundational elements for bringing vitality to your relationship, so it's important that you read about them before studying the 19 Vitalizers. Unity is the ultimate goal of any relationship. You will use "Reflection and Consultation", and "Character Growth" continuously as you vitalize your relationship.

These elements are *big* concepts, so Section 1 is simply an introduction. You will grow to understand them more over time as you practice the actions throughout the guide.

Step 2, Section 2: Creating Shared Values and Vision

Next, please proceed to "Section 2: Creating Shared Values and Vision". Here you will begin to use the first three Vitalizers to prioritize your relationship, clarify what values are important to you both, and discern what your vision is for your relationship. You will examine the concept of commitment and how it assists you to apply Perseverance in creating a relationship filled with vitality.

- Vitalizer 1: Prioritizing Our Relationship
- Vitalizer 2: What Is Important to Us?
- Vitalizer 3: Where Are We Going?

Step 3, Sections 3-6:

Creating Loving Partnership
Creating Connecting Experiences
Forging Deeper Connection
Expanding Beyond Us

After completing the first two sections, you will have a great foundation in place. Look at the remaining sections that include Vitalizers 4-19 in four sections (listed below), and decide how you want to proceed. There are many possibilities:

a. You can study and implement the Vitalizers in numerical order.
b. You can focus on the topics where you feel you have the greatest need for vitalization.
c. You may wish to begin with a topic you already feel quite good at, so you are encouraged to keep going.
d. You may read through all the content quickly and then pick areas to spend more time on.
e. You may spend a few months going slowly through each Vitalizer, and then re-visit the topics for review once a year.
f. Your own approach.

You have your unique couple relationship, and this is a guide for creating a healthy, happy, and unified connection between the two of you. Apply Flexibility in the way that is best for your journey as a couple.

Below are the sections and Vitalizers:

Section 3: Creating Loving Partnership

- Vitalizer 4: Establishing Our Friendship
- Vitalizer 5: Understanding Each Other
- Vitalizer 6: Respecting Each Other
- Vitalizer 7: Loving One Another
- Vitalizer 8: Appreciating One Another
- Vitalizer 9: Unifying Our Communications

Section 4: Creating Connecting Experiences

- Vitalizer 10: Choosing to Merge
- Vitalizer 11: Enjoying Social Time

- Vitalizer 12: Sharing Laughter and Humor
- Vitalizer 13: Giving Thoughtful Service

Section 5: Forging Deeper Connection

- Vitalizer 14: Communicating About Sex
- Vitalizer 15: Managing Our Money
- Vitalizer 16: Growing from Difficulties
- Vitalizer 17: Resolving and Rebounding

Section 6: Expanding Beyond Us

- Vitalizer 18: Establishing Family Unity
- Vitalizer 19: Connecting with Friends and Community

Character and Vitality

Every book about relationships is different, depending on the topic and the expertise of the authors. In this case, we are experts on the topic of character, so you will read introductory material about that and then see the emphasis on character throughout. [See "Core Element C: Character Growth".]

We believe that couples can commit to each other and choose to vitalize the quality of their partnership. If your goal is to create couple vitality and keep your relationship lively over time, this guide will be your companion book that you refer to often. *Couple Vitality* provides actions you can take to quickly make improvements. However, the content is also designed to be a significant and ongoing part of your life.

Enriching Your Experience

You will gain new perspectives as you increasingly incorporate the concepts in *Couple Vitality* in your life. If you include elements of the arts, this can enhance your learning and your relationship. Your activities may include music, drawing, dance, poetry, writing in a journal, photography, or other uses of Creativity to enhance your learning and understanding. Incorporating the arts generates joy and draws you closer together.

From Your Viewpoint As a Couple

You will notice that most of the book is written in the voice of a couple who is deeply engaged in the process of building couple vitality. The pronouns used are ones like "we" and "our". These pronouns invite you to identify with the content, see yourselves as partners, and carry out the behaviors being talked about. "We" is not the authors, who are colleagues and not a couple.

About Timing

Couple Vitality can be useful for couples at any relationship stage when they want to strengthen, grow, or heal their relationship and adopt new behaviors individually and as a couple. It's a learning tool for preventing issues. Couples may also find it beneficial to work with a mentor-couple, coach, or counselor along with learning.

This guide is *not as suitable for individuals and couples in the middle of a major crisis*, such as excessively using drugs or alcohol, in an unsafe situation, or experiencing violence or trauma. These couples will benefit from professional help and healing before attempting to strengthen their relationships, at which point this guide may be useful.

Creating Couple Vitality—A Dynamic Process

About the Model

Achieving couple vitality is a dynamic process that involves the key aspects of couples' relationships. The model below visualizes the major components of this process: the 3 Core Elements and the 5 dimensions of Couple Vitality. The 19 Vitalizers detailed in this book are distributed among the 5 dimensions.

The 3 Core Elements are "Unity", "Reflection and Consultation", and "Character Growth". They represent behaviors that are necessary for the successful practice of every Couple Vitalizer. Unity is located in the center of the model because it is the ultimate goal of any relationship. "Reflection and Consultation", and "Character Growth", are shown as parallel circles on the outside of the model, because couples utilize them continuously as they vitalize their relationship.

The 5 dimensions of Couple Vitality are "Creating Shared Values and Vision", "Creating Loving Partnership", "Creating Connecting Experiences", "Forging Deeper Connection", and "Expanding Beyond Us". These dimensions support each other in an ever-evolving and expanding process that couples apply to dynamically build and strengthen their relationship. The actions couples take as they apply these dimensions unify them and empower them to build a wider unity with children, extended family, friends, and community.

As couples engage in the Couple Vitality process, they achieve the goal of Unity.

The model is shown below.

Creating Couple Vitality
A Dynamic Process

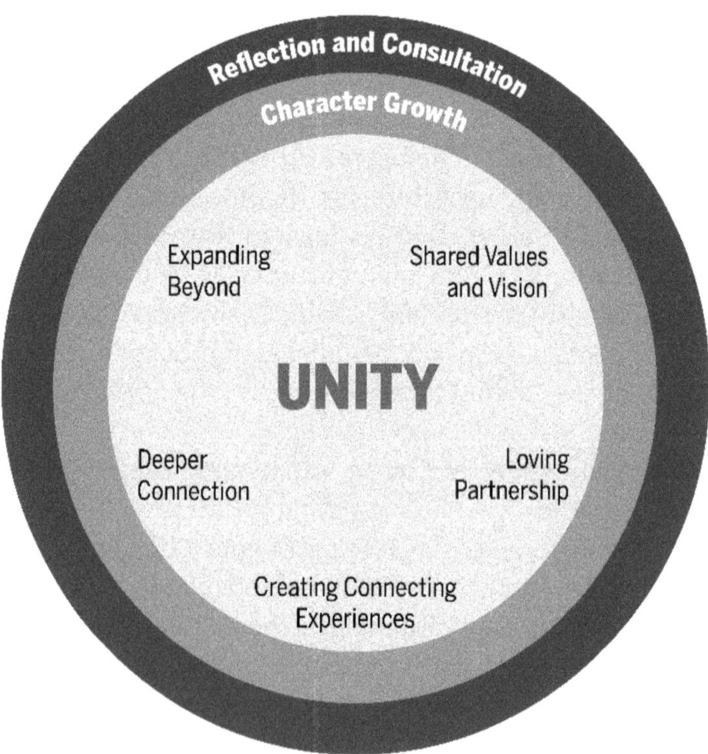

Section 1:

Powerfully Creating Vitality

Section 1 Introduction

Relationships gain vitality when you commit to consistently applying three essential elements. This section introduces you to these elements that you will practice throughout the guide as you focus on the 19 Vitalizers. In this first section, you will learn about the importance of:

- **Core Element A: Commitment to Unity**—Unity is the "glue" that keeps you together and functioning in harmony. It includes being fair with each other and maintaining your connection as a couple. While you will not always agree, when unity as a goal is very important to both of you, it provides a strong impetus for navigating disagreements well. You consider the impact of your words and actions and their potential to create unity or cause disunity, and you choose to communicate and act in ways that build unity.

- **Core Element B: Reflection and Consultation**—It contributes to your unity when you reflect on your words and actions as individuals and assess their effectiveness. Unity also builds when you are skillful as a couple in reflecting and consulting to build understanding and reach unified decisions. These two skills apply to every aspect of your life together.

- **Core Element C: Character Growth**—You may think about your unique personalities and how they affect your couple relationship and interactions. However, you will discover in this guide that your Character Qualities are even more vital to focus on, in part because you have significant power to grow and develop them. When you each have many Character Quality strengths and apply them for the good of each other and your relationship, you will avoid the conflicts that often arise when Character Qualities need significant growth.

The topics here in Section 1 are themes throughout the book. You will have opportunities to build your skill with them in each Vitalizer.

Core Element A: Commitment to Unity

"... [W]ith unity in diversity, we grow together through a true realization of our wider potential and primal oneness."
Raymond and Furugh Switzer

Focus Statement: We strive to create a state of harmony, connection, and oneness in our thoughts, feelings, words, and actions.

Deeper Learning:

All the Parts Contribute

We love the concept of "unity", and we see it as a powerful state for us to strive for in our couple relationship. However, we realize that the concept and our journey to achieve full unity is a complex process.

To achieve a state of unity as a couple, both of us individually practice the Character Quality of Unity. As we include later in "Core Element C: Character Growth", this Quality is defined in this way:

> "Unity is consciously looking for and strengthening points of commonality, harmony, connection, and attraction; accepting and leveraging differences; and working with others to build a strong and coherent foundation for oneness, love, fairness, commitment, inclusion, cooperation, and common goals."

We also recognize that the Character Quality of Reflection and the couple communication practice of consultation are also vital contributors to creating our state of unity. These are discussed in the next chapter, "Core Element B: Reflection and

Consultation". Our ability to reflect on our actions separately and together keeps us honest. Bringing all topics up and consulting about them to build understanding and to make effective decisions keeps us in tune and moving in unity together.

The Vitalizers, which are covered in most of the other chapters of this book, fine-tune our words and actions to have us more consistently live in a state of unity. We contribute to this unity with a common vision, turning toward each other, laughing, socializing with each other, and much more.

[***Note:*** For clarity, the Character Quality of Unity is one of the 22 Character Qualities focused on in the book, and these are capitalized throughout the book. When the book content focuses on the state of unity, the word is uncapitalized.]

Unity and Vitality

We began our relationship as two individuals with separate lives. Our couple journey is about how we come together, what we love and appreciate in each other, and what becomes our shared identity. We, in essence, create something new: our partnership. In that process, we still have our own personalities, characters, and behaviors. We influence these as we interact and connect in our relationship and keep our partnership vitalized.

As we consider how to create couple vitality, the centerpiece is unity. It's the starting point for everything vital and healthy. It may not yet be a common word in our relationship but increasing our focus on creating it will result in couple vitality. Creating unity invites us to view our relationship as being a single unit that cannot be divided. If we associate oneness with our relationship, it shifts our viewpoint and actions in a new way.

With unity, we:

- Place the health and strength of our relationship above self-interest
- Focus on points of commonality and agreement
- Collaborate on all decisions that affect our relationship or family
- Operate with fairness, Respect, and equality
- Feel a deep connection between us

We Are Still Individuals

Of course, we still retain our individual personalities and who we are as people—being united is not about losing ourselves in being a couple. It's also not about agreeing all the time or having everything in common, as different viewpoints can spark new ways of looking at a situation. It's not about dominating each other into an unwilling agreement either. It's about valuing our harmony so that we are motivated to function as teammates and as our best selves. We connect in healthy ways with each other:

> "A healthy marriage is the union of two individuated, differentiated persons. These are people truly capable of loving the uniqueness of each other. Thus, the union of marriage is not ever intended to be enmeshment or unity in conformity, as this would attenuate who we can truly be. Rather, with unity in diversity, we grow together through a true realization of our wider potential and primal oneness. Mindful differentiation always develops through connection, not disconnection."[3] Raymond and Furugh Switzer

Our commitment to unity raises our awareness of when our interactions cause disunity and disconnection instead. As we increase our appreciation for unity and lose our tolerance for disunity, we become more attracted to each other and strive to strengthen our connection. With focus, effort, and practice, we will discover new ways to create unity every day.

Striving for "We" and "Us"

We begin interactions consciously focused on unity, create more unity with the quality of our words and actions, and strive to reach unified outcomes. We practice Dependability in carrying out positive actions and pursuing goals that keep us connected for the long term. Unity keeps our couple vitality growing.

As we strengthen our unity, it becomes easier to carry out the actions that connect us. Our commitment to keeping our unity strong shows in these ways:

> "Research has shown that couples who maintain and act on dedication are more connected, happier, and more open with each other. That's because dedicated partners show their commitment in the following very specific ways...:
>
> - They think more like a team, with a strong orientation toward "us" and "we".
> - They make their partner and marriage a high priority.
> - They protect their relationship from attraction to others.
> - They sacrifice for one another without resentment.
> - They invest of themselves in building a future together—they have a long-term view."[4]
>
> Scott M. Stanley

As we behave like we are teammates on the same "side", we experience feeling united. As we ensure we protect our relationship, contribute to it, and envision staying together, our unity becomes a powerful source of good for us and others.

Science shows the vital necessity of "close connections to other people, and deep connections to moral and spiritual meaning". We are "hardwired to connect". Here's why: "Meeting these basic needs for connection is essential to health and to human flourishing."[5] "Hardwired to Connect"

When we have a secure connection with someone we care about, we are:

- Better at seeking and giving support
- More curious and more open to new information
- More flexible and open to new experiences
- More confident about solving problems
- More likely to successfully achieve goals[6]

Summarized from Dr. Sue Johnson

For us to have unity, we must be strong in the Character Qualities of Truthfulness, Justice, Respect, and Trust. When we apply these Qualities to our choices, responsibilities, and communications, our relationship improves and is protected from harm.

Unity keeps us aware of our relationship's greater context and importance rather than being self-centered. We may also look at the context of our family and community, who look to us as an example of unity. We may have an awareness at times of being part of the greater unity of humanity.

In the next two chapters, we will see new ways of building our unity. In "Core Element B: Reflection and Consultation", we will see how reflecting and communicating with each other increases our understanding and brings us closer. In "Core

Element C: Character Growth", we will learn about how to effectively grow and practice the Character Qualities necessary for creating unity.

Examples:

- Planning a special event to acknowledge a beloved family member or friend
- Waiting to address a problem until the other can be fully involved
- Speaking positively about each other to others
- Practicing Trust with each other to handle agreed tasks
- Stopping actions that are upsetting to the other
- Celebrating anniversaries of special milestones

Applying Character Qualities:

Below are some practical ways to incorporate character into daily practices with the theme of this chapter.

Purposefulness

- Encourage each other to grow and achieve our dreams.
- Collaborate and agree on action steps to fulfill goals and carry them out.
- Support each other's long-term health through planning and cooking nutritious meals and organizing consistent exercise.

Respect

- Listen carefully to each other, paying attention to what is important in each other's lives and offering solutions when invited.

- Speak to each other as adult partners, not in the voice or role of a parent or child.
- Observe, recognize, and utilize each other's strengths and abilities.

Unity

- Share thoughts, feelings, and laughter about what is happening in our lives.
- Turn toward each other to address issues as a team.
- Focus on each other's positive attributes and actions as well as on those of our family members.

Learning Activities:

1. Identify a couple that we think is quite unified. Observe their words and actions and consult with them about how they maintain unity and how they prevent or resolve disunity.

2. Collaborate with planning and carrying out a special occasion in our relationship or family.

Couple Reflection and Consultation:

Throughout this couple guide, there are invitations to practice the Character Quality of Reflection about your interactions and connection. This practice gives you opportunities to celebrate progress and consult to address issues.

1. What would demonstrate that we are unified in our functioning?
2. In what ways does feeling unified affect our well-being and couple relationship?

3. In what ways does feeling disunified affect our well-being and couple relationship?
4. What actions can we take to build unity when our relationship appears to be out of harmony?
5. How could increasing kindness between us influence our level of unity?
6. How do we use laughter or humor to build unity between us?
7. What new ideas for building unity and connection with each other are now coming to mind? How will we carry them out?

Core Element B: Reflection and Consultation

"... [N]ine times out of ten, conflicts may be resolved when couples step into each other's shoes."
Les and Leslie Parrott and David H. Olson

Focus Statement: We reflect on our own, and we use consultation to reflect together and deepen our understanding of each other and various issues, making effective decisions as needed.

Deeper Learning:

Creating couple vitality has many facets, and it will take time for us to collaboratively increase it. It's exciting to learn new ways of developing an excellent relationship, and we will enjoy celebrating our progress and becoming closer.

Two linked communication practices will assist us in our growth process. The first one is applying the Character Quality of Reflection, which we use to gain insights as individuals and as a couple. The second practice is consultation. It will take Perseverance and Excellence to do both Reflection and consultation well, so we will be patient and kind with each other as we learn.

Reflection

Reflection is an opportunity for us to pause, breathe, and gain new perspectives. We use Reflection when we need to consider what we have done, why, and the outcome, something that often requires us to practice Humility. Reflection builds our understanding of ourselves and one another. We can use it as an aid in learning about what did and did not work well. We often use Reflection as individuals, but it can also be done together. Below are some of its elements. We:

- Calmly build self-awareness and understanding as we assess ourselves
- Explore to understand our actions, thoughts, feelings, and perceptions about a situation
- Analyze to gain insights into potential approaches and actions for improving behaviors and circumstances
- Seek inspiration and new insights to address issues and ways to keep creating vitality in our relationship
- Visualize ourselves as a unified entity

When an interaction between us becomes intense and potentially disunifying, we can stop the action and take time to calm down and use Reflection individually. Then we can come back together more peacefully, share our insights, and create outcomes in unity.

As we improve our ability to engage in Reflection, we gain a greater understanding of our motives, goals, personal history, and reasons for reactions. We share our new perspectives and gain further ones as we interact. We also increase our ability to adjust or to completely change our viewpoints and approaches.

Consultation

"Consultation" is a word that can have multiple meanings, so we will learn how it applies to couples as part of the process of creating couple vitality. It's a type of dialogue designed to build understanding between us and to assist us in effectively achieving unified decisions. As with any skill, it takes time to learn, and we will have opportunities to practice it frequently.

Consultation, when we do it well, can significantly increase our harmony and decrease conflict between us. A communication practice like this is particularly useful for us as a couple, as there can be no majority vote like there can be with a group. Consulting together requires us to apply Truthfulness and Trust with each other. These Character Qualities assist us to be vulnerable and share what is on our hearts and minds. Applying Compassion and keeping our words kind when we demonstrate Truthfulness can make it easier to stay connected and build understanding:

> "... [R]esearch shows that as much as 90 percent of marital spats can be resolved if all the couple does is accurately see the issue from each other's perspective. Don't miss this point: nine times out of ten, conflicts may be resolved when couples step into each other's shoes."[7]
> Les and Leslie Parrott and David H. Olson

Consultations may be informal or formal, unstructured or structured, and be quick or take a lot of time. When we both apply Flexibility, we choose the approach that fits us and the issue we are consulting about. Consultation can have elements of formality, such as an agenda or advance fact-finding, especially if we have a major decision to make. However, as we integrate consultation into all aspects of our relationship, we discover how to flow with the process more informally.

We often consult while eating, walking, traveling, drinking tea or coffee in a comfortable sitting area, and more as a couple. Sometimes we start consulting about a topic and then set it aside for time to reflect. Sometimes a quick consultation takes two text exchanges on our phones, and it's done. At other times, we may revisit a topic in person for weeks before it's clear that we are in harmony about a particular decision.

Key Aspects of Couple Consultation:

1. We collaborate as partners to build understanding about what is true for us and/or to make unified decisions.

2. We do our best to have pure motives and demonstrate a Positive Spirit of goodwill about each other's intentions.

3. We are willing to listen with Humility and learn, stay calm and composed, and apply Perseverance through difficulties.

4. We clarify and agree on the topic we are addressing and determine whether we have the facts needed to proceed.

5. We seek to understand each other through careful listening, summarizing what each of us has said as needed.

6. We share thoughts, feelings, and factual details throughout.

7. We contribute equally to the process, which includes freely sharing information, offering opinions for consideration in a calm and composed way, and seeking to understand and gain new insights.

8. We are committed to discovering the truth, which can emerge in many ways, including from different—and even apparently clashing—viewpoints.

9. After we share something, it belongs to neither of us; this central pooling of contributions frees us to practice Flexibility and be open-minded to receive new

information and use it for our common purpose; we merge ideas as appropriate, and we determine together the best outcome.

10. We avoid feeling hurt in the process of fully examining what is true for us, which we assist with a loving and kind atmosphere.

11. We stay focused centrally on what we are creating together, and we do not position ourselves on opposite sides; there is only one side: Our Side.

12. We reach a mutually agreeable conclusion about what we newly understand or about a decision of what is best to do, often something new neither of us thought of before.

13. We carry out decisions and plans in unity; when the process is not going well, we can consult and change direction rather than blaming or criticizing each other or our initial decision.

14. At times, we consult and cannot reach an agreement, and then we make a mutual decision for one of us to take the lead and begin action with the support of the other; we mutually encourage and assist each other while carrying out actions so our unity is protected.

15. We re-consult while carrying out a decision to determine if progress is going in a positive direction or if we need to do something different

Consultation is a process that invites us to come up with inspirational ideas throughout. Sometimes before consulting we use silent Reflection or prayer to welcome these ideas. At times we also invite experts to consult with us, such as for financial planning, or invite family members if a topic involves them. We decide ahead of time if we will get their input and then make a private decision or whether they will be fully involved in making a group decision with us all together.

Consultation requires us to be collaborative, where we strive together to reach positive outcomes. Here is a description of speaking in this way:

> "The tone of collaborative dialogue is friendly. Even when the topic is a serious one, the tone still feels cooperative, as if you have placed your problem on a table and the two of you have sat down side by side to try to solve it. You feel that you are confronting the problem together, rather than that you are confronting each other.
>
> "Another tip-off that dialogue is collaborative is that you feel a sense of forward movement as you accumulate shared understanding. Adversarial dialogue feels repetitious. When dialogue is cooperative, with each successive comment you feel movement toward a shared plan of action."[8] Susan Heitler

We have observed that learning the skill of consulting as a couple is a gradual, experiential, and dynamic process, which does take time. The more we incorporate it into our lives, the more natural it feels, and the more unity we build. No matter how swiftly we learn to carry it out, there will always be times when we need to slow down the pace. This will give us enough time to use Reflection, determine adequate facts, understand and express thoughts and feelings, and fully address an issue.

We appreciate feeling unified, and we increasingly see how Reflection and consultation contribute to our unity. It's becoming clearer that Character Qualities such as Compassion and Respect are essential to our having productive and unified consultations. Character is the next Core Element in this section. In addition, the Vitalizers covered in "Section 3: Creating Loving Partnership" will contribute to the quality of our consultations.

Applying Character Qualities:

Below are some practical ways to incorporate character into daily practices with the theme of this chapter.

Purposefulness

- Turn to each other each day to consult about the issues that arise in our lives.
- Carry out tasks, activities, and projects, determining when we can do so together and when it's better to do them alone or with others.
- Check in periodically to review progress toward achieving our goals and dreams.

Reflection

- Think about and then consult about our words and actions, noting what was beneficial and identifying what we want to improve.
- Consider the Character Qualities we applied and strengthened each day.
- Determine a place where quiet thought can more easily occur and go there each day.

Respect

- Talk with and listen to each other as equal partners.
- Show confidence in and appreciation for what each of us contributes.
- Ensure we address our well-being before and throughout consultations.

Learning Activities:

1. Explore different methods of using Reflection to see what is most useful for each of us under various circumstances. Some ideas might be meditation, writing in a journal, taking a walk out in nature, or asking each other explorative and curious questions.

2. Share some positive memories from early in our relationship. What feelings arise as we reflect on these previous experiences? Is there something we did then that we want to do again now?

3. Experiment with consulting in different locations, with or without another activity happening (examples: walking, driving, cooking...), and with and without physical closeness or touch. Reflect and consult about what we felt was positive, what did not work well, and what we want to try again to strive for improvement.

4. Choose a relatively small topic that we need to address. Pause to reflect on it separately and then together. Then engage in consultation to create a solution acceptable to us. Try out the new solution and reflect on the outcome.

Couple Reflection and Consultation:

Throughout this couple guide, there are invitations to practice the Character Quality of Reflection about your interactions and connection. This practice gives you opportunities to celebrate progress and consult to address issues.

1. What works well for us to say and do before we begin to consult?

2. What topics are easy for us to manage? Which are more difficult?
3. When there are issues that we cannot easily resolve, how do we manage them?
4. Where could we benefit from increased skill-building and practice? For example:
   - Reducing defensive reactions when hearing an idea or opinion
   - Being more open to each other's input during consultations and avoiding criticism
   - Listening effectively and resisting interrupting
   - Increasing Character Qualities of Compassion and Respect
5. When is it useful for us to use consultation simply to build understanding rather than to make a decision?

Core Element C: Character Growth

"The stability of our lives depends on our character."
Frank Pittman

Focus Statement: We apply and strengthen the Character Qualities that we have developed throughout our lives and guide our choices about how to think, speak, and act in beneficial ways.

Deeper Learning:

What Is Character?

We are born with the capacity to develop many positive Character Qualities throughout our lives. As we develop these Qualities, they collectively become our character. These Qualities positively influence our thoughts, words, and actions. The resulting positive behaviors then improve our couple interactions and build our couple vitality.

Each of the 19 Vitalizers in the following chapters will include ways to strengthen and appreciate our Character Qualities. Character growth is a daily activity and ongoing process, so we do our best to be patient with ourselves and each other as we grow.

> "The stability of our lives depends on our character. It is character, not passion, that keeps marriages together long enough to do their work of raising children into mature, responsible, productive citizens. In this imperfect world, it is character that enables people to survive, to endure, and to transcend their misfortunes."[9] Frank Pittman

We each have character strengths, and we each appreciate different strengths in one another. Our feelings of love toward each other are often because we love each other's Character Qualities. When we have talked about which Qualities are most important to us, we have difficulty choosing. However, the Quality of Respect [defined below] is one that we try to have as a consistent practice. Respect assures us that our consultations are positive and productive and fosters the vitalization of our relationship.

Character Quality Definitions

Below is a list of 22 Character Qualities and their definitions. These Qualities are drawn from the Character Foundations Assessment™, a validated instrument developed by author W. Grant Peirce IV. When these 22 Character Qualities occur throughout this book, they are capitalized to draw attention to them.

You are probably familiar enough with the concept of character to notice that this list could include many other Character Qualities, often known as "virtues". This list will guide you for now, and you can certainly over time add other ones to your daily actions, such as patience, encouragement, or loyalty.

Note: Taking the Character Foundations Assessment™ may assist you in understanding your orientation toward each Character Quality and subsequently with implementing the content of this book. You can contact either of the authors to take the assessment and receive an accompanying insights session with either of them or with another certified practitioner. See "About the Authors and Our Contact Information" at the end of the book.

CharacterYAQ Character Quality Definitions
1. **Adherence** is following guidelines, rules, agreements, and laws created to protect relationships, safety, and order; staying faithful to promises made to others, including a partnership commitment.
2. **Compassion** is demonstrating a unique capacity to listen deeply to others about their situations; understanding others' feelings; caring for others' well-being; and seeking ways to ease someone's pain and suffering in mutually satisfactory ways.
3. **Creativity** is drawing on ideas, inspiration, or imagination from many sources to develop or produce something new; being resourceful, intuitive, and solving problems in unique and beneficial ways; and immersing in a problem or situation, looking broadly for insights and connections, allowing for breakthrough ideas and solutions to emerge.
4. **Dependability** is making and keeping commitments, completing agreed tasks, honestly managing resources and money, handling information wisely, and cleaning up after mistakes.
5. **Excellence** is achieving high standards and a superior quality of work, effort, appearance, relationships, and personal development; learning and improving from experiences; and continually raising and meeting expectations.
6. **Flexibility** is being open to change and surprises, adjusting and adapting to life as it happens; being nimble in responding to different people and situations; and considering new and different approaches, methods, ideas, and viewpoints.

7. **Friendliness** is demonstrating an outgoing and positive social attitude; reaching out to connect and build relationships with people; and gracious and warm consideration for others by interacting with polite manners, respectful gestures, thoughtful actions, and honest but kind words.
8. **Honor** is having clear principles, beliefs, and positive intentions that guide actions to create beneficial change.
9. **Humility** is seeing and accepting one's whole self, including strengths, imperfections, abilities, accomplishments, failures, and needs in modest and realistic perspective; offering one's time, knowledge, and talents in a self-effacing way; and being willing to accept the knowledge, skills, and help of others.
10. **Justice** is making careful, independent, and proactive observations of others' actions; initiating decisions, agreements, or actions based on clear facts that are free of bias or prejudice; ensuring fair rewards and appropriate natural consequences or agreed corrective actions occur; and setting appropriate boundaries in relationships.
11. **Moderation** is recognizing and avoiding extremes in use of time, words, actions, and other choices; accomplishing variety, balance, and positive outcomes in such aspects as rest, work, community service, and leisure activities; and effectively applying and adjusting a level of intensity of focus and action to both accomplish goals and protect relationships and well-being.

12. **Orderliness** is living and working with a sense of harmony; creating uncluttered, well-organized, clean, and shareable spaces; developing systems that allow for easy finding; and systematically planning improvements, tasks, and projects.
13. **Perseverance** is applying energy, effort, and resources toward worthwhile goals until achievement is attained; being committed to the long-term future benefit of actions done in the present; and using focused determination to overcome challenges or adversities as they arise.
14. **Positive Spirit** is maintaining a happy, optimistic, and uplifting attitude; energetically celebrating the best in relationships, work, and service; and looking at the positive side of circumstances.
15. **Purposefulness** is pursuing and fulfilling meaningful long-term personal goals, commitments, aspirations, and needs; contributing ideas, words, and actions; and participating primarily in vital activities that contribute to desired outcomes.
16. **Reflection** is calm self-awareness, understanding, and assessment; inwardly exploring actions, circumstances, thoughts, feelings, and perceptions; seeking inspiration; and analyzing to learn the best approaches for improving situations.
17. **Respect** is interacting with all people and what they value with fair treatment, dignity, consideration, and esteem; and recognizing the best knowledge, skills, talents, and abilities of others.

18. **Self-Discipline** is maintaining the inner control to perform needed and important tasks in a timely way; consciously responding in appropriate ways; and choosing what is beneficial or productive and resisting what is harmful or distracting.
19. **Service** is acting selflessly and often sacrificially, directly or indirectly, and with positive intent; and providing time, knowledge, or resources to benefit others without expecting reward or recognition.
20. **Trust** is generously extending confidence; assuming the good intentions and actions of others; accompanying others through learning experiences that build skills and capacities; and giving and expecting appropriate confidentiality.
21. **Truthfulness** is recognizing and accurately communicating facts and feelings; independently seeking knowledge of people, circumstances, issues, and information.
22. **Unity** is consciously looking for and strengthening points of commonality, harmony, connection, and attraction; accepting and leveraging differences; and working with others to build a strong and coherent foundation for oneness, love, fairness, commitment, inclusion, cooperation, and common goals.

Character Growth

We have been very excited to realize that our Character Qualities can always be growing. When something this important grows every day, it becomes a major contributor to our vitality as a couple. We are always becoming our best selves. Character Qualities are different from our personality traits that are set when we are young, and we do not generally try to grow or change them, although we may adjust them at times. [See “Vitalizer 7: Loving One Another” for some content on personality.]

Here is a perspective on the growth of Character Qualities (virtues):

> “Cultivation is an apt metaphor for the development of virtue: the best fruits, vegetables, and grains come from strains of plants that have been carefully developed over a long period and that require special treatment to come to fruition. …Virtues can take root in our lives if we foster them with appropriate care and attention…to become the best people we can be.”[10] Blaine Fowers

We notice that the more we acknowledge how our character strengths contribute to our relationship and home, the happier we both are and the more loving we feel. We catch each other each day doing something positive, and we express our appreciation. It’s like a verbal hug that demonstrates our Positive Spirit and Respect. We become deeply connected. [“Vitalizer 8: Appreciating One Another”, will share more about this.]

Being in a couple relationship provides many signals to us to improve—if we are open to them. It’s in the space of our relationship that we often see our character triumphs and failures. When we struggle with our own or each other’s behavior, we know we have the choice to continually improve and to keep building character strengths. This is a lifetime process of taking action, reflecting on our words and actions, and making changes each day. Our behavior the next day is then more powerful, more life-enhancing, and more beneficial to others.

> "In an unconscious partnership, you believe that the way to have a good relationship is to fall in love with the perfect partner. In a conscious partnership, you realize you must be the right partner. As you gain this more realistic view, you acknowledge that creating a good relationship requires commitment, discipline, and the courage to change."[11] Harville Hendrix and Helen LaKelly Hunt

As we recognize new actions are needed, we can assist each other to grow. For example: One of us may struggle to exhibit a Quality, and this is difficult for the other. Perhaps we act negatively when our partner seems mired in a problem or grief over a heartache. We can then strengthen our Character Qualities of Positive Spirit and Compassion in response. This, in turn, encourages the other partner to strengthen a Quality they were not applying, such as Humility or Perseverance. As we see each other practice various Character Qualities, we can be inspired to improve ourselves. While character growth is primarily an individual activity, it's also an ongoing, dynamic process between us.

Demonstrating Trust and Respect prevents us from attacking each other's character or becoming defensive. Character attacks are among the most damaging actions we can do in our relationship, as they wound the heart and soul.

Research has found that:

"… a criticism is global and expresses negative feelings or opinions about the other's character…."[12] John Gottman and Nan Silver

When we are upset with each other, it can be automatic to use angry and critical words. However, it's more effective to consult about our issues and to focus our attention and words on the positive behaviors and Character Qualities we want to see. [You will learn more about addressing complaints in "Vitalizer 9: Unifying Our Communications".]

Below are some examples of character attacks and suggestions for new Character Quality Language™ to use instead. This is a new language, and in the beginning, it felt strange for us to use it. However, as we consistently practice it with one another, we are seeing its powerful positive effect. [More on this language is in "Vitalizer 8: Appreciating One Another".]

- ***Attack on Dependability:*** "You are so irresponsible and always late."
  Character Quality Language: "Please use your Dependability and be on time for your appointments."

- ***Attack on Justice:*** "You are always unfair to me."
  Character Quality Language: "Please use your Justice and treat me as your equal partner."

- ***Attack on Orderliness:*** "You are very messy."
  Character Quality Language: "I request you use your Orderliness and put away the ingredients after cooking."

A Couple Shares Their Experience: *"Before we committed to each other, we made sure to know our own character strengths and observe each other in real-life circumstances. It's obvious how valuable this was now that we are living together. We both have the strengths of truthfulness and trust, and we are very grateful. However, it can be challenging to create a safe place to encourage and influence one another's character growth. We must be very kind and tactful so that what we say is perceived as positive encouragement and not criticism. We have also realized how powerful it can be to notice and appreciate each other's efforts to apply character qualities in our life together. When we focus more on each other's positive qualities, we demonstrate excellence every day."*

It takes commitment to learn and grow individually and together. With mutual sharing in our relationship, we can influence and support one another, something that contributes to maintaining our love, connection, and vitality. This process of gaining gentle feedback from one another about our characters and actions can then be an ongoing practice. The more we share and consult about our goals, approaches, concerns, and successes, and the more we are connected in this effort, the more potential there is for growth. We are one another's helpmate and partner, and we celebrate our progress together.

Character Pairs

Character Qualities are positive attributes, and when we apply them, we intend to create benefits and positive outcomes. However, we are learning that we can cause harm if we apply a Quality to excess or in the wrong time or place. Often we notice we are most effective when we pair a Quality with a "helper" Quality, and this produces a better, more balanced outcome.

For example, when we pair Compassion with Truthfulness, it protects our unity. We do not speak so frankly with each other that we hurt feelings. As another example, if we want to strengthen our Orderliness, through re-organizing an area of our home, it's wise to use the Quality of Respect to check with our partner first and get their input and agreement.

As we strengthen and encourage each other to consistently practice a full range of Character Qualities, we enhance our ability to be successful at functioning as a unified couple.

Note: If you initially have difficulty turning to each other for encouragement and assistance with character growth, you may begin by turning to a close friend or professional instead. Then you can gradually begin turning to each other.

Examples:

In "Vitalizer 8: Appreciating One Another", you will learn about using Character Quality Language™ for showing appreciation toward one another by including a Character Quality. The examples below begin to demonstrate this practice.

- "I noticed you practiced Self-Discipline and had a great exercise workout this morning. Well done!"
- "Thank you for your Dependability in carrying out our decision to increase unity with your parents. We will have a great meal together."
- "I was happy today that I found our legal paperwork quickly. Your Orderliness has improved so much!"

Applying Character Qualities:

Interestingly, we can also apply certain Character Qualities to the lifelong process of improving our characters. Below are three possible ones for us to use.

Excellence

- Apply the most appropriate Character Quality or action to each unique situation rather than doing what we have always done.
- Take advantage of opportunities to improve when they present themselves and strive to improve each day.
- Hold a high standard of achievement, not settling for "good enough".

Reflection

- Assess words and actions regularly to determine better choices.
- Observe and consider the effect of our words and actions on others.
- Evaluate when to apply more than one Quality at a time for a balanced outcome.

Self-Discipline

- Stay with a personal improvement process until achieving a consistent and positive outcome.
- Focus on the beneficial outcome from personal improvements to keep going forward.
- Choose the Quality that is best in every situation rather than the easiest.

Learning Activities:

1. Carefully read the "CharacterYAQ Character Quality Definitions" in the text above. As we read, listen to our internal response to each one. Pay attention to where we have a positive response to seeing a Quality that is generally a strength for one of us and we appreciate its value in our life. We might also experience a nudge that points one of us to a Quality that could be strengthened. We may also have personal experiences or cultural views that affect our response to a particular Quality, and we may need to re-frame it. Example: The Quality of "Excellence" might seem like it's only driving work performance. However, we can use Excellence in other parts of our life, such as in creating a happy family.

2. We each choose a Quality to focus on developing for an agreed length of time. Consult together to generate ideas of specific actions we could take and goals we could set.

   This may be an effort where using the arts is beneficial. For example, each of us could:

   - Create a drawing or painting of ourselves and include our strengths and the chosen growth Quality in the picture
   - Find photos in publications or online that demonstrate behaviors that reflect specific Qualities
   - Listen to or watch songs, videos, or poems that talk about various Qualities, or create a song, video, or poem

3. Below is a form called "My Character Development Plan". This can provide a useful structure for strengthening each chosen Quality and achieving personal accountability.

Sometimes we may like applying Orderliness with a consistent and structured plan, but at other times we may choose to use Creativity to develop a different or more spontaneous approach. As we each practice our chosen Qualities, we will recognize when we are successful at applying the Quality to a situation and provide positive affirmation to each other. We promise to carry out a celebration of major achievements.

My Character Development Plan **EXAMPLE**
Quality to Develop: *Perseverance*
Why? Because I often fail to finish my personal projects. Too often I allow problems or obstacles to discourage me, and I stop being in action. Sometimes I lose motivation, or I postpone action until "I have more time."
What are the obstacles, barriers, or challenges I face that prevent me from practicing this Quality? I am experiencing some health difficulties that make me feel tired at times. My car has broken down, so it's difficult to get to some of the activities I want to. I am also reflecting on whether I automatically say "yes" to people and do not pause to discern if I have taken on too many personal projects.
Who Can Help or Encourage Me with This? My friend ____ told me they found some strategies for developing their virtue of Perseverance.
Development Goal (Desired Outcome): I currently observe that I am very distracted and unproductive in my projects. If I could stay consistently focused and in action 75% of the

time, I will be practicing Perseverance and completing my projects.		
Development Actions:	**Start Date:**	**Assess Date:**
1. I will create actionable goals and firm deadlines for when to complete 2 personal growth projects. I will make myself accountable to (my friend) or someone else for the delivery of these results.	Date	Date
2. Talk with my friend ____ or other friends whenever I feel discouraged; this will help me to address the obstacles so I can keep moving forward.	Date	Date
3. When starting action on each project, I will take a few minutes to reflect on the importance of Perseverance, focus, and determination.	Date	Date
4. Read inspiring quotations and stories about Perseverance daily and visualize myself persevering as I go through my day.	Date	Date
Signs of Improvement: After 1 month of doing this, I completed 1 of the 2 projects, and I am 75% finished with the second project. I have overcome many challenges that came from my life circumstances and also from a couple of difficult interactions with others.		
New Actions to Take: Keep up my accountability and talk to my friend ____ more often about this—at least once every 2 weeks.		

Note: There is a blank table below that you can use, or you can set up a similar format on an electronic device or in a notebook.

<table>
<tr><th colspan="3">My Character Development Plan
(Use whatever format or method works well for you)</th></tr>
<tr><td colspan="3">Quality to Develop:</td></tr>
<tr><td colspan="3">Why?</td></tr>
<tr><td colspan="3">What are the obstacles, barriers, or challenges I face that prevent me from practicing this Quality?</td></tr>
<tr><td colspan="3">Who Can Help or Encourage Me with This?</td></tr>
<tr><td colspan="3">Development Goal (Desired Outcome):</td></tr>
<tr><td>Development Actions:</td><td>Start Date:</td><td>Assess Date:</td></tr>
<tr><td>1.</td><td></td><td></td></tr>
<tr><td>2.</td><td></td><td></td></tr>
<tr><td>3.</td><td></td><td></td></tr>
<tr><td>4.</td><td></td><td></td></tr>
<tr><td colspan="3">Signs of Improvement:</td></tr>
<tr><td colspan="3">New Actions to Take:</td></tr>
</table>

Individual Reflection:

Throughout this couple guide, there are invitations to practice the Character Quality of Reflection about your interactions and connection. This practice gives you opportunities to celebrate progress and consult to address issues.

1. What are some Character Qualities that I see are strengths of mine? What are the Qualities I am assessing in my behavior and focused on strengthening?
2. What interferes with knowing my character? How can I overcome these challenges?
3. Which Character Qualities could I apply to improve my interactions with my relationship partner and other family members?
4. When have I paired two different Character Qualities to produce a more positive outcome? Which pairings have been most effective?

Couple Reflection and Consultation:

Throughout this couple guide, there are invitations to practice the Character Quality of Reflection about your interactions and connection. This practice gives you opportunities to celebrate progress and consult to address issues.

1. Which Character Qualities do we most appreciate in each other?
2. How does noticing and appreciating these Qualities affect how we feel about each other?
3. When do we rely on a character strength of the other? When is this positive? When do we rely on the other instead of developing the strength ourselves?

4. What are beneficial ways for us to influence each other's character growth?
5. When do we find it difficult to use a character strength with each other? What makes it difficult? Would there be benefits from using it anyway?
6. When do we use a character strength to excess with each other and there is a poor outcome? Is there another Quality that could be paired with it to apply Moderation and balance its use?

Section 2:

Creating Shared Values and Vision

Section 2 Introduction

Here in Section 2, you will begin learning about the Vitalizers that lead to couple vitality. The three Vitalizers here in Section 2 build a foundation for the rest.

As a couple, you form a new entity that has never existed before: your relationship. Even if you have been together for a while, you can "re-create" the quality of your relationship. You empower this process when you use Creativity to develop a vision for what you want and underpin it with the values you both recognize as vital.

The priorities you set and the values you hold as individuals, as well as those that you choose to be important as a couple, influence your relationship and behavior choices. Your shared vision for your life together influences the direction you are going in and the goals that you set to move you along on your life journey.

In Section 2 you will learn about and apply:

- Vitalizer 1: Prioritizing Our Relationship
- Vitalizer 2: What Is Important to Us?
- Vitalizer 3: Where Are We Going?

Vitalizer 1: Prioritizing Our Relationship

"Successful couples are on each other's side.
They view themselves as allies, not adversaries."
Susan Page

Focus Statement: We make it a high priority to arrange for regular time together as a couple, giving one another our full attention and strengthening our connection and unity.

Deeper Learning:

We are faced with many choices of what to do with our time. It's our unified well-being that we realize we must place at the heart of our agreed-upon choices, and this contributes to our couple vitality. We protect the harmony in our couple relationship as we consistently consider how our choices will affect each other and then choose what is best for us both. If instead we focus only on our self-interests, we can put a wedge between us.

If we become overly involved in activities and commitments that take us away from each other, we can begin to lose a feeling of connection, and disunity and distance can arise. This is especially true if we don't come back to each other and talk about our experiences. It's wise to consult periodically about what we are involved in to see if it's wise to apply Moderation to our time and activity choices, so we have more time together. This assessment can include where our time and skills are most needed and what brings us happiness.

A Couple Shares Their Experience: *"We were asked to do 'one more thing' to benefit our community, and we knew if we said 'yes', it would be too much. We both spent time using Reflection and writing down all we were doing and our* *motivations for being involved. We looked at the time we were spending at work and looking after our home. We assessed the effect of our time choices on our couple relationship and our family, and we began to see that we were rarely spending quality time together. We looked at the overall situation, and we determined to make "us" much more of a priority. This detailed process helped us feel more in control of our time and choices. We were able to say 'no' to some things, 'yes' to others, and modify yet others. We committed to time together. What a relief!"*

On the other hand, sometimes we enjoy watching each other immerse in an activity, or we enjoy hearing the stories afterward. When we experience our partner feeling fulfilled and satisfied, it can also bring us happiness. For example, one of us might create art, participate in a team sport, or act in community theater. The other could watch or enjoy the outcome.

Harmonious couple time is a gift to us and those around us, as it contributes to our happiness and love. It's wise to consult and clarify between us what we mean by "couple time". For example, one might think that consulting about a child's needs is couple time. The other might think it's only when we do a social date away from home. The actual activity is less important than whether the time together strengthens our feelings of connection to one another.

Relationship author Susan Page identified the vital practice of couples demonstrating "goodwill partnership"—a consistent way of positively influencing their relationship. She writes:

> "I interviewed thirty-five couples who described themselves as 'thriving.' I thought I might find that they all came from happy, functional families, or that they had

> unusual degrees of compatibility, or that their problems were relatively minor compared with other couples—none of that was true. Some of them had rotten childhoods and enormous challenges. But there was a quality I found in all of these thriving couples that I find is usually missing in more troubled relationships. I now believe that quality is a deeper key to happiness than even good communication or mutual respect.
>
> "It's a quality I call a spirit of goodwill. Successful couples are on each other's side. They view themselves as allies, not adversaries. They want to be happy together, and together they make this happen. In a spirit of goodwill, they accept the traits in their partner that they wish were different. They have given up trying to change each other. When they argue, they understand that a different point of view may be valid. Because they want to experience their love all the time, they would rather work toward a solution than hang on stubbornly to their own 'right' point of view."[13] Susan Page

Ahead in "Vitalizer 3: Where Are We Going?", we will create a vision for our relationship, and we will recognize that achieving our goals will take a significant investment of time. The world is a busy place with many demands on our time. Parenting adds another strong pull on our attention and resources. Distractions and interruptions are common. However, prioritizing couple time is a vital support for our well-being as individuals and our relationship.

When we are unified and happy as a couple, it contributes security and love to our children and enables them to grow, learn, and develop in healthy ways. We are also more prepared to be involved in our work and our community service. Our unity builds, and we feel more alive and connected.

Examples:

- Have a weekly or monthly date night. [See "Vitalizer 11: Enjoying Social Time".]
- Enjoy cuddle time on the couch with dessert.
- Train children to allow a few minutes of mom and dad time each day without interruption.
- Organize an outing in nature with cooperative challenges.
- Text when away from home with reasonable updates about whereabouts and timing.
- Avoid spending time with others who may want us to be unfaithful to each other.

Applying Character Qualities:

Below are some practical ways to incorporate character into daily practices with the theme of this chapter.

Adherence

- Show steadfast faithfulness to each other, respecting any promises or vows of commitment we have made to each other.
- Treat each other's personal information and private activities as confidential.
- Create clear boundaries and agreements for a beneficial plan for improving our relationship and aiming for long-term success.

Moderation

- Assess the effect of our time choices on our relationship.
- Look at the overall balance of our responsibilities and adjust them as needed to protect the unity of our relationship and our well-being.
- Choose to spend leisure time together.

Unity

- Enthusiastically participate in couple activities.
- Focus on increasing sincere harmony while spending time together.
- Identify specific activities that especially increase feelings of connection, appreciation, and long-term commitment.

Learning Activities:

1. Reflect, consult, and agree on times and activities in which mobile phones are turned off or silenced and not responded to. Agree on what could qualify as an emergency interruption that we would respond to.

2. Consult about ways to be in regular contact with each other when apart, try them, and agree on what is effective.

3. Identify an area or activity where we could be more allied with each other and carry out the steps needed to increase unity and goodwill partnership.

4. Plan a time away from home where there can be intimate conversations about wishes and dreams.

Couple Reflection and Consultation:

Throughout this guide, there are invitations to practice the Character Quality of Reflection about your interactions and connection. This practice gives you opportunities to celebrate progress and consult to address issues.

1. How can we know if something is good for us?
2. When have we been effective at having a spirit of goodwill in our relationship?

3. How could we increase our spirit of goodwill toward each other? How could this benefit us?
4. When is it wise to suspend judgment about each other so we don't overreact?
5. How do we view being in communication with each other when apart? How can using Respect influence our choices with this?
6. How can we protect our relationship from harm?
7. How happy or unhappy are we with our amount of couple time? What do we want to do differently?
8. Does our current couple time feel like quality time? Why or why not?
9. How does time on our electronic devices affect our couple time? What is beneficial? What seems potentially harmful? What boundaries or practices do we want to now include in our lives?
10. Are we balancing who does the arranging of couple time? If not, what new arrangements need to happen?
11. How do we feel about watching or hearing about each other's activities or accomplishments?
12. When does spending time with family members also feel like couple time? When does spending time with friends also feel like couple time?

Vitalizer 2: What Is Important to Us?

"We cannot say enough about the importance of staying true to your deepest values and of honoring those of your partner."
Patricia Love and Steven Stosny

Focus Statement: We know our own and each other's high-priority values, and we create our shared values for our relationship and our life together.

Deeper Learning:

Values drive the prioritizing of our time and the reasons for our actions. As partners, we grow from exploring our perspectives and beliefs, and then we form a shared foundation of what is important to us and what outcomes we want to see in our lives. This shared foundation demonstrates the unity spoken of in "Core Element A: Commitment to Unity".

When something is important to us, we use our Honor and dedicate our time to accomplish it. For example, if family unity is an important principle for us, we spend time with our children and other relatives regularly. If we value our work or education, then this is a significant way we spend our time. If contributing to the lives of others is something we value, we engage in various types of community service. If we are motivated by personal growth and spiritual enrichment and community, then spiritually-based activities are important to us. If we value nature and enjoy being outdoors, we spend time there and perhaps live close to a natural environment. If we have ethnic or cultural heritages that we identify with and want to include as part of our life, we will carry out various celebrations, ceremonies, or traditions.

If entertainment is a priority, we may choose to spend our time watching television or movies, attending concerts, playing games, and so on. Perhaps physical fitness is a priority, and we exercise regularly. Social media may be another way we spend our time, using it for connection with others. However, we stay aware when social media and electronic device use becomes excessive and it becomes a barrier between us, instead.

A Couple Shares Their Experience: *"When we began dating, we were both exercising regularly. One of us swam a lot and the other did muscle-strengthening at the gym and rode a bike. We tried exercising together, but it just did not seem to work well. Our bodies needed different activities, and our schedules did not mesh well for exercising. We found after committing to a life together that we both enjoy going on walks, and this is good exercise and couple time. However, we generally still do serious exercise separately. We made a promise to each other to do our best to accomplish some form of exercise daily and let the other know about it. We do not hit this goal 100%, but the promise keeps us in action. We congratulate each other on our achievements. We value being active throughout our lives."*

We gain insights when we use Reflection to examine our core values and consider how they impact our use of time and energy. We sometimes discover discrepancies between what we identify as our core values and where we spend most of our time. For example, we may say we value quality time with each other, but then answer work emails and calls during the evenings and weekends instead of connecting. Where we have values in common, it can be easier to determine our choices and what we see as a larger purpose for our lives. Where we have diverging values, we can sometimes experience conflict or disappointment.

Here is a perspective on the link between values and commitments:

> "Every time we make and keep a commitment to ourselves—large or small—we increase our self-confidence. We build our reserves. We enlarge our capacity to make and keep greater commitments, both to ourselves and to others. ... [W]hen keeping your commitment becomes hard, you have two choices: You can change your behavior to match your commitment, or you can lower your values to match your behavior. One choice will strengthen your integrity; the other will diminish it and erode your confidence in your ability to make and keep commitments in the future. In addition, that shift in direction with regard to values—even if it's slight—will create a change in trajectory that will create a far more significant difference in destination down the road."[14] Stephen M. R. Covey

As we reflect on our values, we will begin to see whether our behaviors show that we value each other and our couple relationship. Do we stay in regular communication? Do we spend enjoyable time with each other? Do we demonstrate Respect in our interactions? Consider this:

> "... [T]here are a few rules I know to be true about love and marriage: If you don't respect the other person, you're gonna have a lot of trouble. If you don't know how to compromise, you're gonna have a lot of trouble. If you can't talk openly about what goes on between you, you're gonna have a lot of trouble. And if you don't have a common set of values in life, you're gonna have a lot of trouble. Your values must be alike."[15] Morrie Schwartz

When we value our relationship, we both believe it's important to thoughtfully meet each other's needs. Demonstrating Service to each other can be a vital component of being a healthy couple. We look at what each other needs to be happy and healthy, and we carry out the words and actions that contribute to well-being to the best of our ability. These will vary according to the stage of our relationship and family and our varying circumstances. [See "Vitalizer 13: Giving Thoughtful Service".]

Our shared values keep our words and behaviors in line with what is important to us:

> "Every time you violate your core values—even if you're just reacting to your partner—you feel guilty. For example, if one of your core values is to be a loving partner and you forget your anniversary, you'll feel guilty. Guilt is the direct result of your beliefs and actions being out of alignment with each other. It's your brain's way of warning you to get back in line with your core values. ... We cannot say enough about the importance of staying true to your deepest values and of honoring those of your partner. If you make this a regular practice, your relationship will not only improve but also be transformed without your ever talking about it."[16] Patricia Love and Steven Stosny

Note: You will find more on the concepts covered in this Vitalizer in "Section 4: Creating Connecting Experiences".

Examples:

- "We value being fit and living a long life, so we exercise regularly."
- "We value our couple and family unity, so we apply Moderation to our time choices with work, leisure

activities, and community service, and we spend quality time at home."
- "We value ongoing learning, so we both read books and take courses, sometimes together."

Applying Character Qualities:

Below are some practical ways to incorporate character into daily practices with the theme of this chapter.

Dependability
- Keep promises to each other in a timely way, using our Character Quality of Trust and creating harmony.
- Align our actions with our shared values.
- Hold and stay faithful to our values with courage and conviction even in the face of pressure, challenge, or temptation.

Honor
- Identify, understand, and appreciate each other's values and how they connect to our shared values.
- Consult and agree on our shared values.
- Actively apply shared values in daily life actions, choices, and decisions.

Purposefulness
- Identify long-term goals that are consistent with our shared values.
- Focus on activities that contribute to achieving our long-term goals.
- Courageously apply our highest values in using and sacrificing our time and energy for positive purposes.

Learning Activities:

1. Individually, list our top five values that underlie our time choices. Share our lists and consult with each other about how these values are affecting our lives separately and together. Consult about whether to adjust how we are using our time and what new actions we commit to.

2. Write a list together of the values that we want to be at the foundation of our couple relationship. Consult about how these values might influence our daily choices. If we have children who can participate, consult as a family about our foundational values.

3. Choose one of our values and create a list of ways we can spend time together to manifest it.

Couple Reflection and Consultation:

Throughout this couple guide, there are invitations to practice the Character Quality of Reflection about your interactions and connection. This practice gives you opportunities to celebrate progress and consult to address issues.

1. How can clear individual and shared values contribute to our life together?
2. How can we determine a set of values that applies to our relationship? To our family?
3. Who else could assist us with clarifying our values?
4. How can we remember our values and apply them when faced with a situation or a decision to make?

Vitalizer 3: Where Are We Going?

"Putting your whole heart into a relationship
is the only way to get maximum value from it."
George S. Pransky

Focus Statement: Our values support and harmonize our vision for our lives together, and our vision gives us a larger picture of where we are committed to going in our lives together.

Deeper Learning:

We contribute to creating our relationship together when we agree on our vision and base it on the values we identified in "Vitalizer 2: What Is Important to Us?". It can be easy to just carry out the day-to-day tasks of life and not see our destination. Developing a vision reminds us to lift our eyes and see a larger plan for our lives. We can look ahead and see the potential fruits of our efforts.

When we picture our couple life—what do we want to see? What do we want to create together? What do we want our relationship to be like? Are we going to raise children? Where do we choose to live? What are we striving for in terms of material well-being? What do we want to achieve with our self-expression and Creativity, and how can this be accommodated in our relationship? How might spiritual elements contribute to our lives? What daily habits will we incorporate?

We may be tempted to focus on: "What do we *not* want?". However, it's wise for us to focus on the positive we want to create, instead. We also need to consider what is changing in our lives, what needs may have shifted, and what is important for us to prioritize.

Change and individual differences affect all relationships:

> "Throughout the marriage husband and wife must make room—even if reluctantly—for change and for difference, for altering values, tastes, needs, and careers. Husband and wife continually confront the issue of how to reshape their shared identity so it continues to express what they want as a couple and what they need as individuals. Given the vast number of choices and trajectories, this challenge creates a never-ending tension in marriage.
>
> "... [I]t is out of this push-pull of autonomy and togetherness that the couple acquires a sense of good emotional, moral, and cognitive fit. To reach the conclusion that the relationship is uniquely gratifying requires the meshing of both partners' conscious and unconscious wishes and needs and the acceptance of compromise as reasonably fair or at least temporarily necessary. To achieve this state, not only must each person feel free to make his or her wishes known but both must agree on what is fair."[17] Judith S. Wallerstein and Sandra Blakeslee

Note: There is more content on fair partnership in "Vitalizer 6: Respecting Each Other".

We have tremendous power and latitude in using Creativity to develop a shared identity and determine our vision. We are creating something new in the world that *has never existed before*. As a couple striving for vitality, our relationship is increasingly greater than simply the sum of the two of us as individuals.

A Couple Shares Their Experience: *"When we were deciding whether to be lifetime partners, we consulted about what we wanted our relationship to be like and what practical actions we could carry out to achieve that vision. When we saw we were in harmony with our vision and what commitments we were willing to make, it became a powerful confirmation that we could confidently go forward. Now every few months we revisit our vision and actions and celebrate when we fulfill our commitments. We also set goals for where we are not progressing and what changes we want to make."*

Using words to state what we are committed to creating or re-creating is powerful. We can think specifically about what is important to both of us and consider the actions that will make our couple relationship more successful. The more specific we are in stating what we want, and in clarifying the actions we commit to carry out, the more we will discover our shared vision and priorities. *This visioning process must not include blaming or criticizing each other for what has or has not happened in the past!*

It takes commitment to fulfill our vision. We stay in our relationship through all its joys and challenges. Keeping this commitment to practice Perseverance involves time, focus, and sacrifice. We commit to ourselves to stay, and we commit to the other person to be there no matter what happens, good or bad. Demonstrating Adherence enables us to maintain our promises and vows to each other. Commitment has us in action to create a couple relationship that is strong, happy, and filled with vital energy.

Below are some perspectives about commitment that calibrate us to its necessity.

"The benefit you get from commitment is peace of mind on both sides. Your partner benefits from knowing you are committed to maintain respect and affinity. He need not fear that circumstance and personal reactions will hurt the relationship. It is human nature for our degree of satisfaction to be tied to the extent of our involvement. Commitment prepares the mind for full involvement and guards against distractions. Putting your whole heart into a relationship is the only way to get maximum value from it. Commitment to a relationship enables you to experience its full potential."[18] George S. Pransky

"Until one is committed there is hesitancy, the chance to draw back, always ineffectiveness. Concerning all acts of initiative (and creation), there is one elementary truth, the ignorance of which kills countless ideas and splendid plans: that the moment one definitely commits oneself, then Providence moves too. All sorts of things occur to help one that would never otherwise have occurred. A whole stream of events issues from the decision, raising in one's favor all manner of unforeseen incidents and meetings and material assistance, which no man could have dreamt would have come his way."[19] W. H. Murray

Once we have our vision clearly stated, we then expand it to include statements of our commitments that will fulfill it. These then guide us when we make choices and decisions. For instance, if we commit to spending time in community service activities, we may choose to forgo another activity and volunteer time with a charitable organization instead. If we are having a conflict between us, then we can look to see if there is a Character Quality or commitment that we are not carrying out with each other or with others. Re-starting what is missing can restore harmony and prevent annoyances and larger disagreements. In other words, striving to fulfill our vision and carry out our commitments creates unity, as we learned about in "Core Element A: Commitment to Unity".

For example, we might write down that we are committed to consulting as a couple at least once a week, more often when possible. Fulfilling this commitment then releases positive energy into our relationship. It's generally harder to criticize or fight with someone when we regularly strive to create unified outcomes. [See "Core Element B: Reflection and Consultation" for more about this.]

As challenges come up throughout our life, we can lift our eyes and remind ourselves of the vision we want to fulfill. When we refer to our written commitments, it empowers us to take positive action. When we are tired, the car has mechanical problems, the bills are due, we disagree about who is going to clean the bathroom, the children are annoying each other, and it all just seems too much, re-focusing on our commitments can restore some of our balance. They remind us of what is most important to both of us, and when we look at them, it prompts us to resume some of the beneficial actions that we may have stopped doing.

As we strive to clarify our vision and carry out our commitments, we will affirm that our relationship is a strong and viable entity. Even if we have been together for a while and experiencing difficulties, we can begin anew.

Applying Character Qualities:

Below are some practical ways to incorporate character into daily practices with the theme of this chapter.

Creativity

- Generate and consider new ideas to incorporate into our vision and commitments.
- Carry out our vision in unique ways.

- Develop concrete displays related to our vision to keep it visible.

Excellence

- Reflect and learn from our experiences.
- Stretch our lives to achieve higher goals and our vision.
- Assess our commitments for fairness and re-balance as needed.

Purposefulness

- Assess our progress regularly using our vision and commitments and re-align our actions as needed.
- Set goals and measurements to keep us moving forward toward our long-term vision.
- Determine a regular interval to reflect on and assess our progress.

Learning Activities:

1. Create a vision statement for our relationship that illuminates our values and what we are striving to create. At this stage, we may know items that we want to write down, but we will let the ideas flow over a few weeks while we study the rest of the Vitalizers.

2. Create a vision board, which is a collage of pictures and words from a variety of sources, or personal photographs, that depict what we want in our life together and for our short- or long-term goals. Visually seeing our goals and desires every day consciously and subconsciously supports us in achieving those goals.

3. Consult about and write down the action-oriented commitments that will assist us to fulfill our vision. Keep adding to them and refining them as we study.

4. Draw a map on a large piece of paper or cardboard and mark the landmarks on it that illustrate our relationship goals.

Couple Reflection and Consultation:

Throughout this couple guide, there are invitations to practice the Character Quality of Reflection about your interactions and connection. This practice gives you opportunities to celebrate progress and consult to address issues.

1. What elements do we envision as essential for a long-term and happy partnership?
2. What habits or practices have we seen other couples use that seem attractive and positive for us to include?
3. Are there dreams or wishes we want to include in our vision, even if we do not know how to achieve them yet?
4. What will assist us to keep our vision visible? Keep us actively engaged in fulfilling its elements?
5. What system will prompt us to periodically review, reflect, and consult about our vision?
6. What do we see as the value in having action-oriented commitments that align with our vision?
7. Are there others who can give us input about our vision and commitments?

Section 3:

Creating Loving Partnership

Section 3 Introduction

Loving partnerships are unique for every couple. Together you will create the ways you maintain your friendship, build understanding, and express love to one another. You will learn about each other's preferred ways of receiving love. You will also stretch into practicing new ways of expressing love to one another. Your ability to demonstrate understanding and love through your words and actions powerfully keeps you connected.

Your connection will increase as you practice the learning ahead in this section. You will focus on the quality of your friendship, learn more about each other, interact in respectful and loving ways, and share communications that show appreciation and build unity. You will draw closer together by developing a partnership between you. Being partners means you are equal in your interactions, collaborative in what you do together, and united in your loyalty to each other.

In Section 3, you will learn more about these Vitalizers and ways to apply them:

- Vitalizer 4: Establishing Our Friendship
- Vitalizer 5: Understanding Each Other
- Vitalizer 6: Respecting Each Other
- Vitalizer 7: Loving One Another
- Vitalizer 8: Appreciating One Another
- Vitalizer 9: Unifying Our Communications

Vitalizer 4: Establishing Our Friendship

"A happy spouse looks at the other person as their best and closest friend—a friend they want to stay close to no matter what."
Shaunti Feldhahn

Focus Statement: We consider each other a close friend, valuing our loyalty, communication, and support.

Deeper Learning:

Having a deep friendship is an important indicator of a high-quality and lasting relationship. Therefore, we are committed to the belief that friendship is a key part of our couple vitality. Using our Honor guides us to keep our friendship strong and healthy.

When we have many shared experiences and activities and have forged a high-quality connection between us, it demonstrates that we are friends as well as lovers. Our friendship and intimacy deepen and strengthen over time and form a lasting foundation for us as a couple.

Being friends means that we are connecting, sharing, and caring about one another. We are in each other's corner, look out for each other, and share most aspects of our lives. We feel safe together, so we can use our Trust to be vulnerable with each other. We are in one long conversation with each other as close friends and companions. We share positive experiences that give us shared memories. We are building intimacy between ourselves as we are connected body, mind, heart, and soul.

A Couple Shares Their Experience: *"Friendship and liking each other is what sets the foundation for us to enjoy each other.*

Friendship helps us communicate and feel drawn to spend time together. We enjoy practicing Service with each other and others around us, and we work toward common goals. We honestly share what we are thinking and feeling. We laugh and have fun together. Our shared history as friends helps us feel connected."

Scientific studies support the emphasis on being close friends:

> "... [H]appy marriages are based on a deep friendship. By this I mean a mutual respect for and enjoyment of each other's company. These couples tend to know each other intimately—they are well versed in each other's likes, dislikes, personality quirks, hopes, and dreams. They have an abiding regard for each other and express this fondness not just in the big ways but through small gestures day in and day out. ... Friendship fuels the flames of romance because it offers the best protection against feeling adversarial toward your spouse. ... In the strongest marriages, husband and wife share a deep sense of meaning. They don't just 'get along'—they also support each other's hopes and aspirations and build a sense of purpose into their lives together."[20] John M. Gottman and Nan Silver

> "A happy spouse looks at the other person as their best and closest friend—a friend they want to stay close to no matter what."[21] Shaunti Feldhahn

Maintaining our friendship is not always easy—it takes commitment, time, attention, and love. Being a steadfast and loyal friend to each other requires patience and the ability to understand, forgive, and get past unpleasantness or disagreements. It also includes recognizing that friendships and relationships go through ups and downs, so there is not just one way for us to interact.

Being friends is one of the best ways for us to feel a strong connection with each other. Consider these perspectives:

> "A simple way to understand connection is to think of it as two people sharing an experience. You touch me, I feel your touch. You talk, I listen, and vice versa. Individuals make connection by paying attention and tuning in to one another—as well as what they are doing. It's as if for a moment there are no barriers between you. Each has access to the other's energy, which creates synergy and intensifies the experience."[22] Patricia Love

> "We discovered that when we help couples change their interactive behaviors—rather than how they feel, think, or remember—they feel connected and begin to have new thoughts and create new memories."[23] Harville Hendrix and Helen LaKelly

A Couple Shares Their Experience: *"Being friends provides a mindset for us to create well-being and form a defense from the harshness in the world around us. We are a safe space for each other to relax."*

Examples:

- Excitedly share about a work accomplishment and respond with enthusiasm.
- Encourage and celebrate each other's progress with difficult tasks.
- Cook a meal while the other is visiting a sick relative, so it's ready when they come home.

- Bring home a book the other would find interesting.
- Share an inspirational video or article.
- Talk about a hope, wish, or dream we have and make plans to accomplish it.

Applying Character Qualities:

Below are some practical ways to incorporate character into daily practices with the theme of this chapter.

Friendliness

- Enjoy time together doing nothing and everything, including relaxation time in the mix.
- Share our innermost private hopes and fears.
- Greet each other with warm and welcoming smiles and hugs.

Honor

- Hold strongly to loyalty in words and actions.
- Look for and appreciate the best in each other.
- Believe in each other's goodwill and integrity.

Trust

- Count on each other to respond when needed.
- Believe we are demonstrating Truthfulness with our words and actions.
- Accompany each other through good times and difficult ones.

Learning Activities:

1. Reflect and consult about our strengths and growth areas for maintaining the quality of our friendship. Consider some of these aspects:

   a. Carrying out honest and kind communications
   b. Enjoying quiet, peaceful time together
   c. Engaging in play, fun, and laughter
   d. Feeling free to be ourselves
   e. Learning about each other
   f. Enthusiastically supporting what is best for each other
   g. Encouraging each other
   h. Staying loyal
   i. Maintaining Trust and Dependability
   j. Sharing interests
   k. Creating common experiences and positive memories

2. Each of us shares a brief story about how a friendship has contributed positively to our lives or is contributing currently.

3. Create a new relaxation activity that prompts us to feel at home and peaceful with each other.

Couple Reflection and Consultation:

Throughout this couple guide, there are invitations to practice the Character Quality of Reflection about your interactions and connection. This practice gives you opportunities to celebrate progress and consult to address issues.

1. What indicates that the two of us are friends as well as partners?
2. How does being friends assist us through difficulties?
3. What encourages us to relax with each other?
4. How does being friends positively influence our relationships with others?
5. What could enhance our friendship?

Vitalizer 5: Understanding Each Other

"...[E]motionally intelligent couples
are intimately familiar with each other's world."
John M. Gottman and Nan Silver

Focus Statement: We strive to pay attention, share, listen, encourage, and understand each other's thoughts and feelings carefully and patiently.

Deeper Learning:

We feel unified when we spend time sharing our inner worlds, listening to one another, and inquiring about each other's viewpoints about matters that arise. This keeps us current with what is happening with each other and assists us to hear the mysteries in each other's heart and mind. We have opportunities to address emotional and practical issues and to encourage each other's activities and dreams. All of this builds emotional intimacy:

> "... [E]motionally intelligent couples are intimately familiar with each other's world. ... They remember the major events in each other's history, and they keep updating their information as the facts and feelings of their spouse's world change. ... Couples who have detailed love maps of each other's world are far better prepared to cope with stressful events and conflict."[24] John M. Gottman and Nan Silver

We know we are each at a different stage of building the skills to achieve emotional intelligence about each other. We have noticed that women are often more comfortable with this type of interaction. However, we have also noticed that men are learning the necessary skills, so we are confident we can keep improving in this area.

Sharing and Listening

We notice that our communications go more smoothly when we are clear at the beginning about our goals or expectations. Sometimes we want to consult to solve an issue. At other times, we just want someone to listen to us. Either way, we appreciate it when our partner is listening, summarizing, and asking clarifying questions. These practices build understanding and show Respect. When we know we have been heard, we feel relaxed, confident, validated, and connected.

With effective listening, we build understanding about what is happening with each other. As we share and listen, we improve the quality of our friendship, intimacy, and unity. Conscious listening, as described below, contributes to effective consultation and problem-solving together, which then reduces or prevents conflicts between us.

Below are three levels of conscious listening:

- *Level One:* Listen for content—Be able to give a concise and accurate summary of what we heard the speaker say.
- *Level Two:* Listen for the emotions—Be able to hear the emotion under the words of the speaker.
- *Level Three:* Listen for the speaker's wants and needs—Be able to hear beneath the words and the emotions what the speaker is asking for and needing.[25] Summarized from Kathlyn Hendricks and Gay Hendricks

Of course, it's also beneficial when the speaker can articulate their emotions, wants, and needs. With our close relationship, we often have a greater sensitivity to one another's thoughts and emotions. Sometimes we can guess what the other is thinking, feeling, wanting, or needing. However, it's unwise to make assumptions without directly asking and listening. Sometimes we can get upset when the other does not "read our mind" and therefore knows what to do for us. However, we realize that the ability to do accurate mind-reading is a relationship myth, and the best principle for us to apply is to use communication and consultation to discover the truth.

Character Qualities such as Self-Discipline and Compassion influence our effectiveness as listeners. Strengthening these Qualities reduces disruption in the process and enables us to better see the topic from our partner's point of view. We stay consciously focused on listening and understanding rather than trying to plan our response or strategize how to fix the problem. We also have the best outcomes when we avoid competing verbally or interrupting.

It takes practice, mutual encouragement, and caring for us to stay tuned in to each other's inner world. Taking the time to do focused listening is a way to practice Respect. We focus better when we set aside what we are doing and eliminate any distractions, such as from our electronic devices. When we tune in to what our partner is sharing, we align our thoughts and feelings and begin to more deeply understand one another.

Understanding Feelings

It contributes to our friendship and the quality of our consultation when we share and understand each other's feelings. They influence how we:

- Perceive the situation we are addressing
- Express our thoughts

- Make decisions
- Create and carry out possible solutions

We improve our life together and reduce conflict when we increase our skills with the factors listed below.

- Stay aware of our current and underlying thoughts and feelings
- Understand what has prompted our feelings, including differentiating between whether it was something from the past, the present, or a mix of both
- Maintain self-control and adjust—not letting the feelings be in charge instead of us
- Be able to express intense thoughts and feelings calmly, clearly, and safely, releasing or calming them through such activities as quiet use of Reflection and prayer, or through constructive physical action
- Understand each other's thoughts and feelings through mutual sharing, and listen patiently throughout so there is space to learn
- Apply Compassion for each other's feelings

Here are some thoughts about how to process feelings:

> "... [R]epressed or suppressed feelings have damaging impact on your health and well-being and this often drives people into counseling or therapy, or they simply fester in unresolved, unhappy, health- and relationship-damaging ways. ...
>
> "What does 'processing your feelings' mean? It means experiencing them, bringing them into conscious awareness so you can feel them, look at them, explore them, think them over, realize insights about them, release them...any or all of the above, wherever the process takes

you. When people experience their feelings in these kinds of ways, they lose their punch. Feelings are transitory by nature. They come…and they go…IF you allow yourself to experience them. But, if you tell yourself any kind of message that blocks your feelings or causes them to get pushed away, they will keep popping up one way or another to grab your attention, sometimes at inopportune times or in inopportune ways. Telling yourself 'I shouldn't feel that way', or, 'I'm carrying on too much about this', or 'I'm being too sensitive', or even, 'Not now' seriously impedes your ability to experience your feelings and may ultimately, make it difficult to access those feelings.

"… [I]f you deny or push aside Feeling A, it's likely to have a negative impact on Feeling B. This is because denial is a primitive coping mechanism, which means that it doesn't simply target the one feeling you want to block off, or lessen, it causes collateral damage to others. So, if you want to have access to happiness and joy and other 'good stuff'…open the door to feeling the tough stuff like loss, sadness, hurt, fear, loneliness, pain, despair.

"So, how do you open the door to experiencing your feelings? The key to giving yourself full access to them is to forgo labeling them as 'good' or 'bad', or otherwise pushing them around in any way: Let them simply be."[26]
Patty Howell

Generally, the quality of our consultations improves when we acknowledge and share our thoughts and feelings about a topic early in the process. Expressing feelings does not mean attacking each other with anger or any other emotion. It does mean saying what feelings are happening and why so that understanding between us builds.

We benefit from recognizing shifting feelings in ourselves and each other as new conversations arise or when situations change. Disunity can occur when we do not acknowledge each other's feelings, we devalue them, or when one of us remains silent and withdrawn for an extended period. Withholding feelings or thoughts and then speaking up later when it's too late to address an issue usually causes frustration and problems. This could include saying things like, "Well, I didn't think that idea would work," or "I felt uneasy about that action" after it occurred.

We remember from reading "Core Element B: Reflection and Consultation" that sharing our feelings and striving for understanding are different than our feelings clashing with each other and conflict escalating. A simple practice can be for one of us to say, "I am wondering how you are feeling about this situation? Can you share with me what is on your mind and heart?" We need to say this with an accepting tone of voice and without accusation or judgment and then allow there to be silence until a response comes. A follow-up practice after speaking can be for the listener to say, "Is there anything else you need to say?" This ensures our partner's inner cup has emptied. We may need to stop at times and summarize back to each other what we think we have heard. When we check for understanding, we quickly correct information and let each other know we are listening carefully.

One challenge with understanding feelings, however, is that we may not yet be skillful with the words to label them. Dr. Marshall B. Rosenberg guides people through the challenges of understanding and identifying feelings. He encourages specificity, which has us state that we are "happy", "excited", or "relieved", rather than saying we feel "good". Being specific contributes to our understanding and clarity.

Some of the words we might use for our feelings when our needs are *being met* are:

- Adventurous
- Affectionate
- Amazed
- Amused
- Aroused
- Calm
- Curious
- Energetic
- Fascinated
- Happy
- Mellow
- Moved
- Optimistic
- Proud
- Relaxed
- Surprised
- Thrilled
- Wonderful

Some of the words for our feelings when our needs are *not being met* are:

- Afraid
- Angry
- Annoyed
- Anxious
- Ashamed
- Bored
- Concerned
- Confused
- Disappointed
- Discouraged
- Embarrassed
- Hurt
- Irritated
- Jealous
- Overwhelmed
- Pessimistic
- Resentful
- Sad[27]

Marshall B. Rosenberg

Sharing Our Feelings

With some practice, we may be able to quickly identify our feelings and name them, sometimes with assistance from each other. Alternatively, we may notice that our feelings only become clear to ourselves while sharing during consultation.

We may easily and intuitively identify feelings, or we may need gentle and exploratory questions to sort them out. Often one or both of us may also need time and space alone to allow feelings to surface and clarify. When we see that we struggle with identifying feelings, it can be useful to write down an incident or situation and then list the feelings related to it, perhaps privately in a journal or with assistance from another person.

It's wise for us to avoid making assumptions or judgments about each other and to simply inquire and acknowledge how each other feels. It's unwise and likely contentious to:

- Tell the other person how they are feeling
- Project our feelings onto the other
- Tell the other that they should or should not be having a certain feeling
- Judge and criticize the other for having the feeling

Our volume or tone of voice, facial expressions, and body movements are also powerful cues about our thoughts and feelings. If we pay close attention, we can begin to observe our own feelings. If we listen carefully, we can also often tell if our partner is feeling upset, happy, angry, excited, or annoyed. When someone's words, facial expressions, body movements, and tone of voice do not align, we will likely believe their tone. It's wise for us to fact-check what we are noticing by asking gentle questions.

As we increase our skill with aligning our feelings and words, our practice of Trust strengthens. When it's strong, it's also easier to offer one another gentle feedback and communicate effectively about our concerns.

How we express and understand each other's feelings can also link to cultural factors or even voice accents. It's also possible that our unique personalities affect how we express feelings, and this causes misunderstandings.

Exploring all these factors together during a calm time may uncover and resolve factors that have been causing us issues.

A Couple Shares Their Experience: *"Over the years there are many ways we non-verbally communicate our love and affection—a look, a smile, a touch—even when with friends. We have learned that the tone of our voice can communicate more than the words we say when we are disgruntled, anxious, frustrated, or unhappy. We have discovered that it's better to consult about an issue when we are in a positive frame of mind. If we are in a negative state, those feelings color the issue. That also gives us time to pray, reflect, and consider options."*

At times what is happening with us emotionally has nothing to do with each other but instead relates to other happenings in our lives. Tuning into our feelings and then sharing that something has triggered feelings and that our partner is not the source, can relax us a bit. Perhaps a neighbor's accident causes some grief related to a family member dying in an accident in the past. Maybe a clerk was rude in a store and anger is simmering. Something happened at work, and there is fear of job loss. We can listen to each other, so we better understand the feelings and let them calm down.

When the feelings that arise are between the two of us instead, it's often more difficult to handle them well. We need to keep practicing so that we can convey our feelings in a constructive way that does not hurt each other. Sometimes we suppress our feelings until the best time, but they begin to leak out in unclear ways that confuse each other. They could also pile up and become an ugly mess when they do come out. It may be useful to at least request some consultation or to have a routine time each day or each week to check in and sort out any issues that have arisen. Sometimes, though, issues arise and must be handled right then.

A Couple Shares Their Experience: *"When we speak, we are aware of how our words include not only the idea we are trying to convey but also how we feel about it. With this awareness, we take time to speak as skillfully as possible, while we also have confidence that our partner will listen attentively. We speak our minds, and we let go of what we have said.*

"As we listen proactively, we are aware of our internal reactions, arising thoughts, and feelings. However, we also know that the process of consulting allows time and space for us to share what each of us feels is needed and helpful. This allows our minds to stay relatively quiet while the other speaks. We can truly hear what is being said as we consider our own opinion and formulate a response.

"Our consultation is then a process of being aware of our feelings as we speak and as we listen. There is a sense of great support in knowing that our marriage partner is openly aware as we do this. For example, I recently returned home from a week-long business trip. My wife was exhausted from caring for our sick four-year-old son for three days.

"When we had a few minutes to sit and catch up with each other and consult about what would happen the next day, we needed time to share our feelings. My wife said, 'I was very scared I was going to have to take him to the hospital without you here'. She added, 'I was so upset that you did not call last night to check on us'.

"With mindful listening, I was able to acknowledge her feelings of loneliness and fear about handling this challenge on her own, without jumping into being defensive. She could then hear me as I shared, 'I was very frustrated that there was not a cell phone signal along the route we were driving last night'. I

went on to say, 'I was very concerned about both of you and hoped you could feel my prayer support'.

"Listening to each other's feelings helped us reconnect. We also realized that we were both too tired to consult about plans for the next day. All we needed right then was to agree on how to look after our son for the next few hours."

In this story, the couple was effective because they were able to share their feelings without interruption. Each was able to listen without immediate judgment. Each was detached enough to realize that they would have to continue the consultation later when they were not so tired.

When we reflect and consult about our feelings, here are some steps that we find useful to follow:

1. Acknowledge and name the feelings we are experiencing
2. Determine what has likely caused the feelings
3. Assess or consult about what to do about the feelings using questions like these:

    a. Is there action to take?
    b. Is there a problem to address with someone?
    c. Are the feelings coming from an old situation and once recognized that they are not part of the present circumstances, can they be released?
    d. Is there physical activity to do that will release and calm the feeling so it's easier to think about it and address it?
    e. Do we need to give ourselves some time to understand what we are feeling and why?
    f. Is the feeling causing us or others harm?
    g. Is the feeling brief and temporary, or has it been with us for a while and needs help from others?

Sometimes we must apply Perseverance when consulting with each other. We take the time to understand each other, increase our emotional intimacy, and build our unity. Understanding then becomes part of the culture of our partnership:

> "When a spouse accurately understands their partner's situation, feelings, and motives, conflicts are curbed. Intimacy increases. Misunderstandings are few and far between. Two people who read each other well, who are enjoying mutual empathy, have more laughter and less bickering. They offer more care and comfort. They have fewer hurt feelings and more fun. They are less judgmental and more perceptive. They indulge each other's quirks. They find more patience for one another. More forgiveness. An abundance of grace and gratitude. In short, more love."[28] Les and Leslie Parrott and David H. Olson

Note: Additional information on understanding your personalities, expressing love, and providing emotional support is in "Vitalizer 7: Loving One Another". Additional information on communication is in "Vitalizer 9: Unifying Our Communications".

Caution: It's important to get assistance when your feelings and interactions are seriously troubling and unresolved. There is a difference between feelings that arise normally every day or you have an occasional annoying interaction, and when the emotions are deep, serious, and stay for long periods. These are likely best addressed with a mental health professional.

Examples:

- Share about a need to participate in a vacation.

- Explain the challenges occurring in beginning a new job, project, or task.
- Express concerns about a child.
- Share grief about a loss.
- Show concern about each other's well-being.
- Understand something from the past that is being triggered in one or both of us and focus on the present situation instead.

Applying Character Qualities:

Below are some practical ways to incorporate character into daily practices with the theme of this chapter.

Compassion

- Pay close attention to nonverbal cues such as hand movements, facial expressions, and eye contact to potentially reveal hidden emotional reactions; verify and do not make assumptions about what is happening.
- Make a conscious effort to identify and consider each other's situation and point of view.
- Demonstrate deep caring and kindness toward each other's well-being.

Perseverance

- Strive to understand each other's thoughts, feelings, and perspectives by asking questions and listening until the communication comes to a natural end.
- Share and consult about our thoughts, feelings, and perspectives with each other freely and regularly to gain and maintain mutual understanding.
- Throughout consultations, even when disagreements arise, focus on the overall goal or core values we wish to achieve and strive to achieve a unified outcome.

Reflection

- Listen carefully to each other and think about the words and feelings shared.
- Pause to seek inspiration and think carefully before sharing thoughts and feelings.
- Search for information to clarify our thinking, analyze our options, and be thorough in our consultations.

Learning Activities:

1. Choose an issue that is causing us some challenges and take turns sharing back and forth about it, with the listener summarizing periodically to check for understanding. The goal is to apply Compassion to understand each other's views, not necessarily to solve the issue currently. If speaking to each other is causing us difficulties, we can sometimes try writing down our thoughts and sharing them that way, going back and forth as needed.

2. Identify the specific positive and negative feelings that could arise in each of the situations listed below:

   a. There has been an injustice in our neighborhood; in our workplace; in our country
   b. We go out on a date to a concert for our anniversary
   c. We have been asked to carry out a specific act of community service
   d. One of us burns and ruins a special dinner
   e. One of us is participating in a spiritual practice, and the other is not
   f. We take our first vacation in five years
   g. We unexpectedly receive a large sum of money
   h. We become parents (or grandparents)

3. To expand our skill in identifying feelings, think about two different scenarios from our life, and then practice a few times using these types of phrases: "When I see or hear ____ (or when ____ happens), I feel ____."

4. Create a "love map" (Idea Source: John M. Gottman and Nan Silver): It's important and potentially vitalizing for couples to know one another well through observing, sharing, and listening. The goal of this activity is to map out our partner's life as we know them now. Then we will fill in the gaps together—without making negative comments about what each other was not aware of.

   Each of us begins with our own piece of paper and some writing or drawing utensils, and we will do the first part of the activity individually. On the paper, we will use Creativity to describe our partner in words and drawings in whatever way works for us. We could draw a tree, squares, circles, pictures, or anything else that displays our partner's life and then add words to it. Here are some examples of topics, in no particular order, but we can go beyond these as needed:

   - Who they are striving to be
   - Feelings most easily expressed
   - Feelings most difficult to acknowledge and express
   - Wounds in the middle of healing
   - Upcoming events
   - Views about children and parenting
   - Profession(s)
   - Favorite activities, community service choices, and high priorities for spending time
   - Best friends
   - Current fears, stresses, and worries
   - Common irritants

- Purpose(s) in life
- Philosophies/practices of parenting
- Life dreams
- Religious/spiritual beliefs and activities
- Basic philosophy of life
- Favorite music, games, movies, TV shows, apps...
- Most special times in life
- Childhood traumas/stresses
- Major aspirations and hopes
- Likely actions if receiving a large amount of money unexpectedly
- Preferred actions to re-charge energy
- Ideal vacation setting

Example: One person could draw a circle for "Current fears, stresses, and worries", and then list in the circle about their partner that they are concerned about: "Adjusting to their new job and their parents' health". The partner could draw a circle for the other showing their "Most special times in life", and then write in the circle: "The couple vacation we took last year and tutoring a teen to succeed in school".

Reflect and Consult: When we have both completed our maps, share them, consult about them, and add to them.

- What were the surprises?
- What did we appreciate learning?
- Were we able to share and learn without becoming upset that our partner did not know something significant about us?
- Do we feel confident we know one another better? That we know one another well?

Related Activity: Now draw a map together of our couple relationship. Consider reflection questions such as these:

a. What are our goals as a couple?
b. What activities do we do together?
c. What do we do separately with agreement from the other, and how do these activities enrich us and our relationship?
d. What roles and responsibilities do we carry out as parents or grandparents?
e. What are the primary relationships we have with family members? How healthy are these relationships?
f. What significant concerns are on our minds and hearts?
g. What are the joys we feel?

Couple Reflection and Consultation:

Throughout this couple guide, there are invitations to practice the Character Quality of Reflection about your interactions and connection. This practice gives you opportunities to celebrate progress and consult to address issues.

1. How can we increase our ability to identify and express feelings?
2. What feelings are most difficult for us to admit we are experiencing?
3. When do we need time alone to reflect before sharing what is on our minds or hearts?
4. When is it unwise for us to immediately express our feelings out loud to each other?
5. What feelings do we especially want to know about when the other is experiencing them?

6. What helps us experience safety when being vulnerable with each other and expressing feelings?
7. What are some ways we can stay current with each other's life? What frequency is needed?
8. How does understanding each other well contribute to our friendship and relationship?
9. What would demonstrate to us that we are skilled with emotional intelligence and emotionally intimate as a couple?

Vitalizer 6: Respecting Each Other

"Each of us has 100 percent responsibility
to create our connection
because we are each whole beings."
Kathlyn Hendricks and Gay Hendricks

Focus Statement: We show Respect to each other as equal partners in our relationship, share decision-making, and appreciate each other's contributions toward our well-being in all aspects of our lives.

Deeper Learning:

When we function in partnership, we demonstrate Respect for each other's abilities and efforts. We create a balance, where we treat one another equally as worthy and noble human beings. We value one another's body, mind, heart, and soul. We show Respect for one another's character strengths, talents, and skills. We appreciate and champion each other's education and career accomplishments. We are grateful for each other's actions in support of our home and family. We strive to understand, value, and practice our cultural heritage(s). We listen to and celebrate each other's accomplishments. We function together as a team.

We use Justice in our relationship, which empowers us to treat each other fairly. We strive to eliminate any patterns of unequal power, domination, aggression, and control over each other. We address areas where growth is needed and where we discover any imbalances. We are then more able to practice Service with each other and share power and responsibilities. [See "Vitalizer 13: Giving Thoughtful Service".]

Consider this:

> "In couple relationships … the well-being of each partner is supported equally, both in the short and long term."[29] "Marital Equality"

As we strive to create an equal and respectful partnership that contributes to couple vitality, we ongoingly consult about our roles and responsibilities. These may be different for each of us and yet still we are equal partners.

We reflect and consult about our experiences to learn what tasks or roles are best for each of us and how we can assist each other. We pursue learning opportunities to expand what we can contribute. We assess the models we learned from growing up or that operate in our friends or families, and we are conscious about what we imitate or eliminate. We examine our expectations of what each other does and how actions are carried out to ensure we are not imposing unreasonable standards on each other. We consider fairness as we carry out activities of all types and as we create our home environment and manage household tasks.

A Couple Shares Their Experience: *"It's both fun and funny to look back on our early years and realize just how much we have both changed as our relationship has matured. We are far from the days when either of us is concerned with spending a few dollars without consulting the other person, just as we are far from the days when we felt that we both needed to be active and equal participants in every aspect of everything. Today, we are both deeply invested in raising our children, cooking, cleaning, developing and managing the budget, and so forth, but we no longer attempt to be equal in the tasks themselves. For us, we are equal at the strategic level and allow for differences at the tactical level.*

"When new issues crop up or we need to support the regular maintenance of our big decisions (examples: parenting approaches, budget development), we are both equally and actively engaged. But for day-to-day implementation, we each have our strengths or otherwise have areas that are just logistically more straightforward for one person to address than the other.

"On those infrequent occasions where we can enjoy a 'day in the life' of our partner, it's much easier to appreciate the many things that the other person does that we would not otherwise even think to notice. If both parties are striving to contribute to the whole to the best of their ability, then the breakdown of specific tasks will fall out where it's most appropriate. This delineation is generally along the lines of each partner's preferences and skills."

Our equality and practice of Respect influence how we make decisions and who initiates actions. We consider all aspects of decisions that affect our lives. [See "Core Element B: Reflection and Consultation".] When we communicate, our tone of voice, the words we use, and our body language all convey Respect.

We rely on each other for advice and wisdom. We build mutual understanding, determine our desired outcomes, and carry out actions together. We share our dreams and consult about our goals. We are fair and thoughtful and not self-centered:

> "It took us a long time to realize that relationships only exist between equals. Each of us has 100 percent responsibility to create our connection because we are each whole beings. People get into trouble when they stop acting from full creative participation. If you take less than 100 percent responsibility, it's easy to feel that other

> people are at fault. … [T]rue responsibility is not about finding fault or accepting blame. It is about a genuine insight into the causes of an action or event. … When true responsibility is taken, learning can take place."[30]
> Kathlyn Hendricks and Gay Hendricks

With equality as a foundational principle, we can function as loving friends and partners. This physical, mental, emotional, and spiritual partnership is vital for us to create a vitality-filled relationship that is happy and lasting. Behaving with equality also provides a healthy model for our children and families. We are true companions to each other.

Examples:

- Consult about what roles we each carry out within the home and family and adjust them as needed to create greater fairness.
- Consult on work choices outside the home or carried out in a home office to determine whether we are meeting our needs and whether the structure we have is respectful and fair.
- Identify a talent or ability in each of us and express appreciation or encouragement to develop it further.

Applying Character Qualities:

Below are some practical ways to incorporate character into daily practices with the theme of this chapter.

Justice

- Assess our roles and responsibilities for fairness and make changes as needed.

- Courageously request consultation when there appear to be unequal or disrespectful actions occurring.
- Challenge each other and consult when something happens that appears to have bias, prejudice, or unexamined assumptions about roles.

Respect

- Demonstrate confidence in each person's voice as a vital contribution to a mutual decision.
- Value each other as truly equal human beings and communicate and act in ways that demonstrate this.
- See each other as functioning in balanced and equal partnership, even when in different roles.

Trust

- Count on each other to carry out our agreed actions, without controlling or micromanaging each other.
- Demonstrate confidence in each other's abilities and judgment through deferring and delegating as appropriate.
- Share honestly with each other the thoughts and motivations related to topics and plans under consultation.

Learning Activity:

1. Identify an area of our couple interactions where we are usually consistent at practicing equality and fairness and expressing appreciation to each other.

2. Choose and carry out one or two projects cooperatively. Take into consideration the strength of our relationship, our physical well-being, and our emotional states to

discern whether an activity is likely to be constructive or rather cause conflict. Below are some ideas.

- Arranging books on a bookshelf
- Gardening
- A camping trip/travel in nature
- Rearranging or decorating a room
- Readying a vehicle and packing for a trip
- Building something for the home
- Putting a puzzle together
- Taking care of a friend's child
- Cooking a meal
- Cleaning out and organizing a cupboard, drawer, or closet

Reflect and Consult:

a. How well did we complete the tasks?
b. How well were we able to cooperate and help one another?
c. Were either of us overly helpful to the other? What was the response?
d. How did we handle differences of opinion?
e. Did we need to involve others in support? Were we in agreement about their involvement and roles?
f. Were we able to listen carefully, demonstrate Respect for each other's input and actions, complete the tasks successfully, and end the project in unity?
g. Did we consult about anything from our lives during the project that we may not have talked about as easily in another circumstance?

3. Look at our furniture and decorations and consult about how they contribute to our lives and demonstrate our

Respect for ourselves, our beliefs, and our cultural heritage(s). Consult about any changes we will make.

4. Identify a talent or skill that one of us has that we have not been drawing on or appreciating and begin to use it or show appreciation for it.

5. Think about couples we have known in the past, have in our lives now, or have observed in a book, movie, or other media. What are some ways they demonstrate equality and fairness between them? What examples do we want to follow?

6. Identify and consult about an area where we have not been practicing equality and fairness as much as we would like. Make a concrete plan to address what we identify as issues.

Couple Reflection and Consultation:

Throughout this couple guide, there are invitations to practice the Character Quality of Reflection about your interactions and connection. This practice gives you opportunities to celebrate progress and consult to address issues.

1. What are our beliefs about equality between partners? About how to demonstrate Respect between partners? Are we open to incorporating these concepts into our life as a couple? Why or why not?
2. What are some of our experiences of practicing partnership, companionship, and equality in our life together?
3. How do the Character Qualities of Justice and Respect affect unity between us?

4. What different roles do we each have? How do these affect our perception of equality happening in our relationship?
5. What can ensure that our behaviors within our relationship and family demonstrate fairness and equality? How do our incomes affect the balance of equality we experience?
6. What skills are we willing to learn that would increase our ability to expand beyond what might be traditional roles and responsibilities? How will we learn and apply them?

Vitalizer 7: Loving One Another

"I am convinced that keeping the emotional love tank full
is as important to a marriage as
maintaining the proper oil level is to an automobile."
Gary Chapman

Focus Statement: We ensure we have loving thoughts about each other and express loving words and actions to each other as contributions to sustaining our loving feelings for one another.

Deeper Learning:

Throughout our relationship, feelings of love attract us to one another. We feel love on many levels, physically, emotionally, mentally, and spiritually. As our relationship grows and we make efforts to connect on all these levels, our love grows into a deeper, more satisfying experience. We do not distinguish between being "in love", "cherishing", and "loving each other"—these are all aspects of a growing and expanding love that unifies us.

Expressing Love

As we strengthen our ability to think loving thoughts, share loving words, and carry out loving actions, the quality of the love between us strengthens. Love is a key element in our being emotionally supportive of each other, and this leads us to feel a close bond of unity while still maintaining our individual selves. In a loving environment, we can be vulnerable and intimate with each other. Demonstrating Trust and Compassion increases our emotional support for each other and our love for one another.

Some people use the word "cherish" when describing how they love their partner:

> "When we cherish our partner, we feel that they're irreplaceable. We simply cannot imagine our lives without them, even when times are rough. We find ways to tell them that we appreciate them, and do that often. This builds trust in the relationship. Cherishing and commitment go together, but they're different. Commitment is really a verb because it is the actions we take daily to let our partner know we are with them, and that we make decisions with them in mind."[31]
> Mary Beth George

As we experience each other's loving words and actions, we grow in our understanding of what communicates love to us. Dr. Gary Chapman has written books about five love languages with the theme that our partner's chosen method of loving expression affects our ability to internalize the message as loving. He says:

> "I am convinced that keeping the emotional love tank full is as important to a marriage as maintaining the proper oil level is to an automobile. Running your marriage on an empty 'love tank' may cost you even more than trying to drive your car without oil."[32] Gary Chapman

Below is a summary of the Five Love Languages from Chapman's work with examples of how to practice them:

1. "**Words of Affirmation:** verbal compliments; words of appreciation, praise, and encouragement; kind words; expressions of appreciation for the other's positive qualities and actions.

2. "**Gifts:** tangible objects freely offered; gifts of any size, shape, color, or price; gifts that indicate thoughtfulness; visual symbols of love with no strings attached and no attempt to cover up a failure or apologize; unexpected gifts, not just on special occasions.

3. "**Acts of Service:** things done willingly for the other; offers of helpfulness; timely and positive response to requests (not demands) of the other; acts of kindness; favors done with a loving attitude (not fear, guilt, or resentment); acts that demonstrate equality and partnership.

4. "**Quality Time:** being available; doing something enjoyable and interactive together; giving uninterrupted, undivided, and focused attention; participating in quality conversations in which both talk and listen; creating memorable moments; intimate revealing of self.

5. "**Physical Touch:** loving (never abusive) physical contact at appropriate times and places; tender hugs, touches, or pats on the arm, shoulder, or back; back or foot rubs or massages; kissing; holding hands; holding while comforting; intimate touch and sex."[33] Summarized from Gary Chapman

When we match our expressions of love with what each other most wants and needs to receive, it can establish or restore our unity. Most partners want to meet the emotional needs of the other, but we may lack the knowledge and skills to be as effective as we want to be. [There is an activity later in this chapter to help you better understand these concepts.]

A Couple Shares Their Experience: *"We kept going round and round with complaints about each other. We were both frustrated and unhappy. One of us felt criticized most of the time. There were no positive words. The other kept feeling lonely and emotionally abandoned. Reading 'The Five Love Languages' saved our relationship.*

"It took practicing perseverance for us to go in a better direction, but the answer was quite simple. One of us needed to receive the Love Language of hearing many positive 'words of affirmation' to feel loved. Any critical words then had twice the negative impact. The other one of us needed the Love Language of 'quality time' that included undivided attention and time together. We looked at our schedules and commitments and made some important changes to have that time happen. With both of us giving each other the preferred Love Language, we are much happier today."

Here is more about nurturing love as a couple:

> "You cannot make yourself feel love or make another person love you, just as you cannot create your own heartbeat. Loving feelings grow and flourish naturally in the presence of certain conditions, in the presence of loving behavior. To behave in a way that nurtures love, you must feel worthy of giving and receiving love. ...
>
> "It is not unusual for loving feelings to be covered over by hurt, anger, resentment, or fear. At such times, love feels dead or absent. Conflicts are the result of natural differences between partners, but most people do not know how to handle conflicts well. Painful emotions or deadness to love is a sign of partners handling conflicts poorly. Hurt, anger, resentment, or fear can last for years if not dealt with. When you feel other intense emotions, you will not feel love at the same time. The unpleasant

> emotion must be attended to properly so that healing occurs, which allows the flow of loving feelings again. Most often, love only feels dead, but is waiting, ready to come to life with the hope that conflicts can be resolved. ...
>
> "A happy marriage needs a mixture of intimate feelings and loving commitment. Loving commitment is determination and resolve that the loved person should flourish."[34] Sandra Gray Bender

There are times when we get into the habit of assuming that we love each other and do not pay attention to expressing it explicitly. We might think, "My partner knows that I love them, otherwise I would not have chosen them, and I would not stay with them." It can be beneficial for us to reassure each other that we love and care for each other—especially when raising difficult issues.

In times of difficulty, old messages from our pasts when we felt unloved or abandoned emotionally or physically can prompt us to feel insecure. An expression of love at that time brings us back into the present, builds security, and demonstrates our Trust. Additionally, when we regularly express loving feelings, they thrive and contribute to our sense of being vitally alive in our relationship.

Note: More on understanding and expressing feelings is in "Vitalizer 5: Understanding Each Other".

Emotional Interdependence

As individuals, we must balance being emotionally connected and interdependent along with being somewhat independent. We must be mature enough to function effectively on our own if we must, but we also choose to be partnered and function together as a whole, healthy unit. As with the two wings of a bird, both of us are unique, with neither the left nor the right one the same, but both are essential and ideally both similar in strength.

As we learn how to live with each other as loving partners, we draw on each other's unique strengths. If one of us is emotionally weak, needy, or overly dependent, we cannot "fly" effectively. If one of us is overly strong and dominant, again the "flying pattern" is uneven, or flying fails altogether. It benefits us to engage in personal growth, have honest and ongoing communications, turn to each other to meet our primary emotional needs, and do our best to demonstrate equality in our actions and attitudes.

In "Becoming Your True Self" we found this view about the importance of achieving this balance between us:

> "The loving capacity includes not only the ability to love but also the ability to be loved—to attract love. We cannot have lovers without loved ones. If we do not know how to be loved or cannot accept it, then we frustrate others who are struggling to develop their capacity to love. Not accepting someone's love is very frequently experienced as rejection and does untold amounts of damage...."[35]
> Daniel C. Jordan

Loving Our Personalities

To be able to demonstrate Respect and love to ourselves, we must know ourselves, and that includes understanding our personalities. Personality is a pattern of thoughts, feelings, and behaviors that make each of us unique. Our personalities may affect how we approach being with and communicating with others, organize our possessions and activities, approach planning and completing tasks, give or receive complaints, control our emotions, and many other behaviors. Consider this perspective:

> "... [O]ur personalities play a central role in our love lives. Personality traits, for example, shape how we communicate and how we like someone to communicate with us. Personality shapes how we give and receive affection, whether we tend to show up early or late, and whether we like routine or variety."[36] Les and Leslie Parrott and David H. Olson

We look at personality and character and see how they are different. Personality is a fundamental aspect of our uniqueness, and we know our personalities were clear at an early age. They were part of what attracted us to each other. Our personalities may have changed a little over our lives and that will likely continue, but very slowly. However, our Character Qualities are vital for us to develop throughout our lives. We can choose to improve each Character Quality when we are aware of our behaviors and their effect on others.

Personality can have a significant effect on our characters. For example, a person whose personality includes being a strong "extrovert" may develop the Character Quality of Friendliness more quickly than a person who is a strong "introvert". However, while Friendliness may come more naturally for an extrovert than an introvert, an introvert can develop this Quality just as fully as an extrovert. In fact, an introvert may develop Friendliness even further than an extrovert because they value interacting with a smaller number of people, and they may have identified it as a challenge and have intentionally focused on and developed that Quality.

We should understand each other's personality traits and love ourselves and each other for them. When we understand each other's personalities, we can better adjust to each other and promote harmony. Our Character Quality strengths apply to the expressions of our personality traits, so they have a positive effect on others.

Here is an example: One of us is more introverted and needs time alone to recharge energy, and the other of us is more extroverted and loves time with people. We practice Moderation and Flexibility so that we both have opportunities to recharge. [See "Core Element C: Character Growth" about loving each other's Character Qualities.]

Examples:

- Express love in the other's favorite way of receiving it.
- Share something that we love about each other.
- Choose and give a card that expresses our loving feelings.
- Do something that contributes to each other's well-being in a way that uniquely comes from each of our personalities.

Applying Character Qualities:

Below are some practical ways to incorporate character into daily practices with the theme of this chapter.

Compassion

- Ensure we understand and help meet each other's needs, even when our perspectives or way of thinking about the matter are different.
- Strive to see each other's perspectives, understand each other's feelings, and consider each other's well-being in our responses.
- Create loving and caring time for each of us to listen to and share our feelings.

Positive Spirit

- Focus our thoughts and attention on what we love about each other and not on each other's faults.
- Express loving feelings in words and actions daily or as often as possible.
- Respond with joy to each other's expressions of love.

Service

- Assist each other to understand and manage emotions, such as love, and express them effectively, beneficially, and consistently.
- Show consistent loving words, actions, and support to each other.
- Seek expert knowledge or professional assistance as needed for us to achieve a high-quality relationship.

Learning Activities:

1. Go to the https://www.5lovelanguages.com website and use the assessment there to determine the ways we both prefer expressions of love from the other. [An alternative is to obtain one of the 5 Love Languages books by Gary Chapman.] Consult about a few simple ways to improve our expressions of love and begin carrying them out. Reflect on and consult about what is working well and where a shift in direction is needed, without becoming critical about what has not happened in the past. It can be beneficial for us to carry out all five Love Languages, but we strive for consistency with at least each other's primary Love Language.

2. What are five aspects of each other's personality that we appreciate? Consult about a new way that one of our personality traits can benefit the other or other people.

What is one aspect of each other's personality that challenges us at times? What Character Qualities or approaches would help us accept and adjust to these more difficult traits? Apply these for an agreed period and then reflect on the outcome.

Couple Reflection and Consultation:

Throughout this couple guide, there are invitations to practice the Character Quality of Reflection about your interactions and connection. This practice gives you opportunities to celebrate progress and consult to address issues.

1. What are our favorite ways to express love to one another?
2. What are our primary and secondary "Love Languages"? What are some of the best actions for us to take to meet each other's need for feeling loved?
3. What mutual way could we express love at the same time?
4. What negative feelings are interfering with feeling loving? How can these be addressed and resolved? [See "Vitalizer 17: Resolving and Rebounding".]
5. When do we feel the happiest? What makes it easier for these times to happen?
6. What do we see as some of the similarities between character and personality?
7. What do we see as some of the differences between character and personality?
8. What are personality traits we each have that we could draw on to enliven our life together?

Vitalizer 8: Appreciating One Another

"… [A] person needs to ramp up the positives so the good-to-bad ratio doesn't fall to a risky level. Couples in solid, lasting relationships do this naturally."
Tara Parker-Pope

Focus Statement: We use positive words of appreciation to acknowledge the helpful contributions and thoughtful actions we each bring to our relationship, family, and home.

Deeper Learning:

Our sincere and loving words have great power to influence and encourage one another. They focus us positively on what we each contribute and lead us to stop magnifying each other's faults. Encouraging words can inspire us to move in positive directions and apply Creativity and Service to achieve goals, try new activities, and much more. When we feel self-doubt, encouragement gives us the courage and confidence to move forward. Encouragement increases our vitality.

Often, we may automatically look for what does not go well rather than what does. It's often easier to criticize than to see and appreciate what each of us does well. However, we must have multiple positive interactions with each other for every negative one:

> "In real life, no couple can keep a running tally of positive and negative displays. There are hundreds of them that happen in any given day. But in a practical sense, the lesson is that a single 'I'm sorry' after bad behavior isn't enough. For every snide comment or negative outburst…, a person needs to ramp up the positives so the good-to-bad ratio

doesn't fall to a risky level. Couples in solid, lasting relationships do this naturally. Sometimes the positives are spoken. 'You look nice today, honey.' 'That color looks good on you.' 'What a great meal.' 'You're a good dad.' Sometimes the positives are gestures—pats on the hand or back, a hug, a tousle of the hair, a kiss for no reason."[37]
Tara Parker-Pope

Saying positive and constructive words increases our Respect for each other and builds our self-Respect, one of the keys to happiness. These types of words lovingly soften our hearts and prompt us do our best with our actions.

When we use *Character Quality Language™* as a specific skill to affirm Qualities in each other, it builds love, appreciation, and happiness between us. This outcome is especially likely when we are sincere and include specifics about the actions each other did. Here are some simple examples:

- "Thank you for your Flexibility in changing your appointment when I needed you to take me to work."
- "I admire your Perseverance! You had to ask your manager for a pay increase several times before they agreed."
- "I love how you show Compassion when your friends need help!"

It takes practice to look consciously for each other's positive actions and speak specifically about them, but it's worth the effort and very affirming for both of us. Having someone notice our use of a Character Quality encourages us to continue behaving positively. Using character words recognizes the gems of each other's heart and soul.

We have also learned that if we follow positive statements with "but" and then say a complaint or criticism, we wipe out any positive effect from the initial statement. The negative comment also seems to cause more hurt when it follows a positive statement.

A Couple Shares Their Experience: *"I am sick with a cold and have been sneezing and coughing. Everywhere I turn, there is a tissue box, waiting for me to cover a sneeze, cough, or drippy nose. I am REALLY grateful to my partner for all these tissue boxes, and they made me wonderful soup, too. I have repeatedly thanked them for their Compassion and Service in taking care of me so well."*

Often, it's beneficial for us to consult and determine how we will apply Character Qualities to a situation, such as Friendliness, Compassion, Justice, or Creativity. Then we can observe how applying them improves it. We also do our best to acknowledge others for their positive behaviors throughout resolving the situation.

A Couple Shares Their Experience: *"I believe that it's especially important to look for opportunities for appreciation during times of difficulties. We recently went through a period with many things going wrong with our home, work, and vehicles. We had to apply creativity to come up with solutions and then use purposefulness and perseverance in carrying them out. Friends and family helped us through all of it, and we saw their faces light up when we shared with them the character qualities that we saw them use to help us. We are grateful to them for accompanying us so well."*

Appreciating each other shows we are grateful for who each other is as a person and the contributions each of us makes to our relationship, home, and family. Expressions of appreciation are great, even when one of us does an agreed task or role, as these positive words provide encouragement and loving support. Gratitude benefits our couple relationship and generates joy:

> "At home the only currency exchange is how you and your mate express your feelings about each other, and gratitude is an often-overlooked commodity. It's easier to say 'Thanks' when you're feeling good about your marriage. It's harder when you're dissatisfied. But gratitude, and its expression, is not just a reflection of a happy marriage; it is one of the causes."[38] Paul Coleman

A Couple Shares Their Experience: *"My partner had a very difficult first marriage. Now that they are in a better situation with me, they say they never want to take me and everything I do for us for granted. They thank me for even the little things. If I hand them a towel, cook a good meal, buy household supplies, consult with them about their work, and so on, they usually say, 'thank you'. I feel appreciated and more willing to participate fully in our relationship. It also reminds me to thank them for all they do!"*

As we reflect on our lives and behavior, we can be grateful for our growth. Perhaps we were able to apply Flexibility when a friend wanted to make different plans. Maybe our child had a difficult day and we applied Compassion through listening well and offering encouragement. We discovered we were able to apply Friendliness with a difficult relative or neighbor. When we see each other's successes in these types of circumstances, we can celebrate and appreciate each other's progress.

Gratitude and thankfulness are similar:

"Without thankfulness people would stay focused on negativity. They would do nothing but whine and complain. They would miss the beauty of life and the power of learning, especially during difficult times. ... No matter how difficult or dark things become, there is always light. There is something to learn in every painful situation. In fact, sometimes when you look back at a really hard test in your life and realize what you learned, that is when you feel the most grateful of all."[39] Linda Kavelin Popov

Examples:

- "Thank you for using Creativity to cook a great meal."
- "I am grateful for your Dependability in managing our finances."
- "I appreciate your Purposefulness in planning learning activities for our children."
- "I love how we applied our Unity when we painted and decorated our home together."
- "You are such a great neighbor! The ways you demonstrate Respect toward us brings us happiness."

Applying Character Qualities:

Below are some practical ways to incorporate character into daily practices with the theme of this chapter.

Justice

- Observe and acknowledge each other's positive actions.
- Stay loyal, refusing to speak negatively about each other to others.

- Provide continual support to each other and help us succeed at the greatest level possible.

Positive Spirit

- Show enthusiasm and appreciation for each other's contributions to our relationship, home, and family.
- Celebrate anniversaries, each other's accomplishments, and when we achieve significant relationship milestones.
- Experience and express thankfulness to each other for the connection between us.

Truthfulness

- Recognize and honestly acknowledge the abilities, gifts, and talents each of us brings to our relationship.
- Use sincere words to share about what is positive and what is challenging as we strive for couple vitality.
- Acknowledge the character strengths each other applies to our lives.

Learning Activities:

1. Take turns practicing the skill of Character Quality Language™ and acknowledge each other for something that we did recently. Reflect together on how it feels to receive such positive words from each other. Begin with one acknowledgment a day and then strive to increase the frequency until it feels natural and becomes part of the culture of our relationship.

2. Each day for a week, share three things we are grateful for. Continue this practice if it's positive and effective.

Couple Reflection and Consultation:

Throughout this couple guide, there are invitations to practice the Character Quality of Reflection about your interactions and connection. This practice gives you opportunities to celebrate progress and consult to address issues.

1. How does it feel when we encourage each other? How do we respond?
2. How does it feel when we show appreciation or gratitude to each other? How do we respond?
3. If we receive appreciation is for doing tasks that we view as a routine part of our role with each other or in our home, do we respond differently? Why?
4. When we have more positive interactions than negative ones, how does it affect our relationship? Our well-being?
5. Are there any recent accomplishments that we want to celebrate? How will we do this?
6. What are we grateful for in our relationship? Our family? Our home? Our friends? Our community?

Vitalizer 9: Unifying Our Communications

"When two people are communicating heart-to-heart, they always feel more respect and caring afterward than before they spoke."
Richard Carlson and Joseph Bailey

Focus Statement: We stay thoughtfully aware of each other's well-being, striving to begin and carry out interactions while demonstrating Compassion, Respect, and Self-Discipline.

Deeper Learning:

It's often a challenge for us—and every human being—to communicate smoothly. We gain our experience with communication from our families, friends, and teachers while growing up, the culture around us, and through relationship experiences. Sometimes we build positive skills, and sometimes we learn poor habits.

We may be happy at times with our interactions, and at other times not so much. Our skillfulness directly affects the quality of our lives. When our words lead to disunity and pain, our stress levels spike upward. However, when our communications build unity and understanding, our stress levels are lower and we feel more connected and happier.

Communication is a broad topic, and we read materials, watch videos, and access other helpful resources so we improve. In this Vitalizer, we focus on preventing some of the ways we can get into difficulty and learning some of the positive skills that aid us.

Caring for Our Well-Being

Important or sensitive communications tend to happen better when we reflect ahead of time about what we are going to say, how we will deliver it, and when we will raise the topic. We can assess the timing or content of what we want to say to see if it would cause harm instead of creating benefit.

It's also wise to address our own and each other's physical, mental, emotional, and spiritual well-being first. This prevents our words and tone of voice from being unnecessarily negative. We can use the tool called H.A.L.T., as it prompts us to apply Compassion, Respect, and Self-Discipline. We can stop or postpone (halt) our communication and address our needs as much as possible:

- **H:** Are we **H**ungry? – Have something to eat
- **A:** Are we **A**ngry? – Take time to calm down and re-center
- **L:** Do we have **L**ow Energy? – Recharge with time alone or time with others
- **T:** Are we **T**ired? – Take a rest break or sleep

When we take a H.A.L.T. break, we can also take time to assess if our ego is in the mode of wanting to be "right" about something, and we need to instead create space for true consultation.

A Couple Shares Their Experience: *"We use H.A.L.T. as one way to proactively avoid conflict. However, we have noticed that when we are using it regularly, it can indicate there is a systemic issue that we need to address. For example, we noticed that one of us was so constantly tired from a long daily work commute that there was regularly no energy to connect or consult. Issues got postponed so much that resentment and conflict started to be common. It could not continue that way.*

"We organized our life and children so that we had a few hours to reflect and consult about the issues we had postponed and about what could change the patterns. We considered all the options and concerns and ended up deciding to move closer to the work location. It was a major upheaval and change, but the quality of our relationship and family life has significantly improved."

Sometimes we may get into difficulty by going forward with a consultation when a pause break or even sleeping overnight would be better. Pausing can be kind, merciful, and gentle with one another. We pause when we notice that we are no longer listening and participating effectively, or when either of us is experiencing a significant escalation of feelings. Indicators may be anger or being flooded with physical symptoms of stress. Letting the symptoms subside for 15-20 minutes makes it easier for us to re-engage in the consultation.

If taking a break results in one of us leaving the home, it's positive to practice Respect and provide the information about where we are going and how long we will likely be gone. It's also wise to agree on which of us will reinitiate consultation and when, and then do so without reminding.

We have various ways we calm our feelings. Sometimes physical activity is a good approach—separately or together—such as exercising, fixing something, or cleaning. Alternatively, we try listening to music, meditating, listening to a positive podcast, watching an uplifting video, spending time in nature, writing in a journal, or praying. We reflect during the break or when we resume, using questions such as these:

- What feelings and thoughts happened inside of me that led to my negative behavior?
- Were they rooted in my resistance, judgments, or fears?
- Was my ego involved—did it get bruised by something?

- How might I have handled my feelings more skillfully?
- Would it have been possible to see what was going on as it was happening, and show Compassion for both of us at that time?
- Are there things that I or we can do now to make this type of behavior or reaction less likely to happen in the future?
- Are there warning signs or remedies that I or we can identify for preventing future issues? Is there a way we can lighten up our interactions effectively, such as by using humor?
- Is there a quotation, prayer, or some simple self-talk that I could use to defuse a situation or feelings as soon as they begin to escalate? For example: "Okay, it's time for me to breathe deeply and to calm down now."

Being Kind and Respectful

When we are thoughtful, gentle, and kind as we begin communications, we are more likely to maintain a unified connection between us. If we begin with an attack and use harsh and critical words, a constructive consultation is unlikely to happen. As the communication progresses, applying tact along with our Truthfulness is vital. We may be frustrated or even angry about an issue we are consulting about, and our thoughts and feelings are important to share. What is essential, however, is always caring about our unity and the integrity of the bond between us.

As we consistently speak from our hearts and practice Respect, our communications will become increasingly harmonious. Here is a goal to aim for:

> "Communication that comes from the heart has the ability to transform. Heart-to-heart communication helps us get past our separate realities to the common ground of

> mental health. It helps our thinking evolve and helps us see issues in a different perspective. When two people are communicating heart-to-heart, they always feel more respect and caring afterward than before they spoke."[40] Richard Carlson and Joseph Bailey

As we talked about in "Core Element C: Character Growth", here again, is this reminder:

> "You will always have some complaints about the person you live with. But there's a world of difference between complaint and criticism. A complaint focuses on a specific behavior or event. ... In contrast, a criticism is global and expresses negative feelings or opinions about the other's character or personality.... Statements that contain complaints are soft start-ups, while those that criticize are harsh start-ups."[41] John M. Gottman and Nan Silver

A Couple Shares Their Experience: *"We are gaining more understanding about how we respond to situations and the ways we communicate. Often, we see we are unskillful because of what we learned from poor communications between our parents. These insights are helping us make conscious choices to respond better. We are seeing occasional times when we can lighten up and laugh, and this diffuses tension. We have also started to realize that focusing on negatives does not always improve the situation. In other words, awareness of problematic forms of communication does not seem to be as helpful as time spent talking about what would be better, and how to achieve it."*

Effective Dialogue

We began to learn about sharing and listening in "Vitalizer 5: Understanding Each Other". Now we are going deeper into strengthening our skills:

> "In the case of dialogue, with conscious effort we can choose to stay with the experience our partner is describing—even though it may feel like a blow to us—without becoming defensive, even if the events being described contradict our memory of them. This does not mean that we agree with what our partner says or how she or he remembers events. Rather, we are staying in our partner's world, disciplining ourselves to stay present and see things as he or she does, according to the way he or she remembers things. Everybody makes sense in their own world, and the feelings they may have are legitimate. Listening well, therefore, puts us into the supportive position of being able to validate our partner's feelings. What they share with us in these dialogues is of vital importance if we desire to be intimately connected to them.
>
> "In order to keep our attention on our partner, it may help to internally 'mirror' everything they say, to get and feel their meaning. We can take this even further and, at intervals, verbally repeat to them what we are hearing, or at least the essence of it, and ask them if we are 'getting it'. This outward mirroring, or paraphrasing, not only clarifies for us that we are understanding them as they want to be understood (which is what listening is all about); they receive the added comfort and feeling of safety of knowing that they are being heard. This helps and enables them to go deeper into their experience, revealing even more of their world to us, bringing a closer and more

intimate connection. It also helps the sender to understand themselves better and perhaps gain a new and objective perspective of their own feelings as they hear them mirrored back."[42] Raymond and Furugh Switzer

Below is a summary of some pointers for positive sharing and listening experiences that demonstrate Trust and Dependability.

Before Starting

- Make sure the listener is available and attentive before beginning to speak; ask, "Is this a good time?"
- Minimize distractions like electronic devices or children having immediate needs

Ways of Communicating

- Start communications softly and gently
- Set aside biases, prejudices, and judgments
- Place Compassion in the forefront of our minds and hearts, so we can be truly understanding of our partner's inner world and life experiences
- Apply Compassion and Respect when asking questions to discern and understand the speaker's words, needs, feelings, fears, and concerns; one method: "We do this by asking cup-emptying questions starting with 'what,' 'when,' and 'how'—never 'why,' which puts each other on the defensive."[43] (Linda Kavelin Popov)
- Apply Self-Discipline to patiently listen
- Listen attentively, summarizing understanding back to each other and clarifying the communication as needed

- Express caring and love as appropriate, sincerely encouraging the other's sharing by using positive facial expressions, physical gestures, and brief words
- Speak for oneself instead of the other
- Interact in partnership and as teammates, working with a shared effort toward discerning truth and understanding one another better
- Sincerely affirm and demonstrate Respect toward the speaker using positive and acknowledging words

Challenges

- Avoid words, tones of voice, or actions that communicate control, domination, or an adversarial position
- Take pause breaks when communication escalates toward dissension, arguments, or conflict, and resume at an agreed time and place
- Set new goals for learning how to communicate and act with one another in improved ways

Despite all good intentions and hopes for a peaceful relationship or home, we may be challenged at times with difficult or hurtful communications. Each of us must apply Self-Discipline and Respect to govern our words and related behaviors. We can effectively observe how we either contribute to harmony or cause disunity. We remember that we are two adults and not parents to each other. As we observe our interactions, we can see where improvement needs to happen.

When Words Bring Disunity

It's especially important in maintaining our couple vitality that we avoid any character attack, severe criticism, or stubborn insistence on our own opinions, as these cause disunity. If these behaviors occur during conversations or consultations, they will interfere in achieving a positive outcome. Studies with couples at The Gottman Institute have observed some highly damaging behaviors that couples carry out at times. These are listed below.

1. **Criticism:** Delivers negative words about personality or attacks the character of a partner; for example, "You are so irresponsible."
2. **Contempt:** Shows disregard through body language, sneering, sarcasm, patronizing, or self-righteous words; for example, "You are such an idiot! You cannot do anything right!"
3. **Defensiveness:** Reacts with resistance and blames the partner; for example, "I am not! You are always picking on me!"
4. **Stonewalling:** After repeated negative interactions, withdraws to avoid communication, thereby shutting the partner out.

When we experience these four negative patterns, especially the first two, we can react at times with "flooding", a protective reaction where physical symptoms such as increased heart rate, higher blood pressure, sweating, and so on overwhelm (flood) us for about 20 minutes, and effective communication shuts down.[44]

Summarized from John Gottman and Nan Silver

The Better Marriages organization recommends this approach below when anger arises between a couple.

1. "STOP! Do not attack. Anger creates defensiveness...and encourages counter-attacks, causing anger to increase and spread beyond the immediate issue.

2. "LOOK! Acknowledge anger. Couples make an agreement to view anger as a normal emotion. Each partner then agrees to acknowledge anger rather than suppress it, and to share how they feel with the other as soon as possible. Sharing is done with an 'I feel' statement.... Clarify with your partner how you interpreted what happened.

3. "LISTEN! Look behind the anger. Anger is typically a secondary emotion. The feelings labeled as anger are often deeper feelings—hurt, taken for granted, trapped, used, overloaded. Couples must look behind the anger...and deal with these other feelings if they are to manage anger. ... When you get angry, consider these questions: What happened just before the incident? What else was I feeling (fatigue, hunger, frustration, overwhelmed, insecure, etc.)? Did this situation remind me of something in my background? Looking behind the anger may not be possible until emotions have 'cooled'. It is hard to think clearly and sort out feelings in the heat of a conflict. Silence or a 'time out' can be useful for a short period. But be careful that silence is not used as a weapon against your partner! Refusing to talk increases anger rather than resolving it. When tempers have cooled, partners can take turns stating what each is feeling while the other listens without interrupting. In this way, feelings can be clarified and heard."[45] "Creative Use of Conflict"

[See "Vitalizer 17: Resolving and Rebounding" for more assistance with this topic.]

Reducing Defensiveness

Sometimes we automatically get defensive when we hear a complaint or our partner raises an issue for consultation. However, we know that reaction makes it difficult to reach understanding and problem-solve. If we notice defensiveness beginning during any interaction, we can:

- Take a deep breath and release it slowly
- Recognize there is an opportunity to listen and learn by saying, "Can you tell me more about this?"; "Please help me to understand."; or something similar
- Summarize what we think we are hearing and understanding
- Clarify as needed

We can use wording that keeps us in learning mode and is less likely to trigger defensiveness. Below is a useful communication practice when we reflect together after trying new behaviors:

- "What worked well for me was ____, and I appreciated it very much."
- "What did not work as well for me was ____, and here is what might work better." Or, "Could we please consult about other solutions."

This "X-Y-Z Formula" may also be useful when there is a complaint:

> "In situation X, when you do Y, I feel Z. So instead of making a critical comment about [her husband's] driving, [a wife] learned to say, 'When we are driving down 4th Street with the kids in the back and you speed up to make the light, I

sometimes feel like making the light is more important to you than our safety.' This simple way of phrasing a complaint is far less likely to cause problems than saying, 'You are such a reckless driver!'"[46] Les and Leslie Parrott

Reducing interactions that prompt defensive reactions, and stopping defensive reactions quickly, both assist our communications to proceed, build understanding, and reach effective conclusions.

In everyday interactions in our home, when we become aware—perhaps after unhappy words—that our partner is struggling with fatigue, overwhelm, or some other difficulty, we can prevent conflict with a constructive response. The recipient of the unhappy words could practice Compassion, take a deep breath, not become defensive, and say, "How can I help?". Then after some time of helping, communication can proceed.

Other Positive Approaches

As we have learned about and experimented with different ways of having honest and peaceful communications, we discovered the "Nonviolent Communication" method. It's designed for people to share and receive observations, feelings, needs, and requests. The example below demonstrates "I-statements", where the speaker is careful to speak for themselves and not be accusatory with statements starting with "you". A simplified view of the basic communication process is:

- SEE: We observe and share the concrete actions in another person that affect our well-being.
- FEEL: We identify and share how we feel about what we observed.

- NEED: We notice and share the needs, values, desires, and so on that led to our feelings.
- REQUEST: We communicate (not demand) a specific request of the other person that is clear and positive that if they carry it out will enrich our life. [To learn more, see Marshall Rosenberg, *Nonviolent Communication: A Language of Life*; https://www.cnvc.org/.]

Here is an example: "I am noticing that you are getting involved in a lot of sports and exercise activities, and I appreciate your commitment to your health. I am concerned though that we are spending less time together. I am feeling lonely and missing you and feeling frustrated that many tasks at home are not being done. I value our relationship, and our children benefit greatly from your time and attention. I request that we consult together before you pursue activities outside our home, so we can ensure together that we use Moderation and achieve balance." A solution-seeking consultation can then follow.

Here is some encouragement about couple consultations:

> "After the sender has conveyed all that is in their heart around the issue and has been heard and mirrored by the receiver, if the receiver then wants to respond to things that have been said, a conscious shift of roles is appropriate. This can go back and forth several times, if necessary, but it is important not to get muddled about who is in what role, so that listening is always taking place, protecting the safe and sacred space between husband and wife from the destructive effects of arguing back and forth.
>
> "In summary, the goal of receiving is to understand completely the truth about what the other is experiencing, sensing, understanding, feeling, associating, remembering

or fearing, and/or what she or he usually does when having such feelings, **and** to convey to the other with words, body language and tone of voice that we are 'getting them', that they are making sense (because all feelings are real and legitimate and everybody makes sense from their own point of view). A further goal is to be able to imagine how they are feeling and to empathize with them."[47]
Raymond and Furugh Switzer

If we reach an impasse in coming together reasonably, it may be wise for us to use outside assistance. We ensure that anyone we involve is strong in Dependability and will not take sides between us. Family members, for example, may find it easy to side with one of us.

Note: It's essential to receive professional assistance when feelings and interactions are seriously difficult and unresolved. There is a difference between feelings that arise normally every day, or you have an occasional annoying interaction, than when the emotions are deep, serious, and stay for long periods. These are likely best addressed by a mental health professional.

Examples:

- "I love how much care you put into this project—could I please make a suggestion about it?"
- "I am concerned about something, could we sit and talk?"
- "I can see you are exhausted and hungry—I suggest we eat, relax, and talk later." [Example of H.A.L.T.]
- "I apologize for trying to force a resolution. I would like to hear your ideas for addressing this issue."

Applying Character Qualities:

Below are some practical ways to incorporate character into daily practices with the theme of this chapter.

Compassion

- Know what is sensitive or hurtful to each other and proceed with care.
- Stay aware of each other's experiences, fatigue level, and stress, and adjust our approach as needed.
- Reassure each other of our caring, even while raising difficult issues.

Respect

- Maintain kindly and courteous tones of voice when talking with each other.
- Appreciate and affirm the strengths and positive attributes in each other, even while raising difficult issues.
- Listen attentively, summarize back what was said, and use appropriate body language to show we are engaged in the consultation.

Self-Discipline

- Pause before acting and speaking to think clearly about what message to deliver and then move forward deliberately and with care.
- Resist interacting based on negative feelings, look ahead to potential negative consequences of starting an interaction harshly, and apply Moderation to our approach and words.
- Calm our emotions, voices, and body language at the beginning and throughout communications to encourage feelings of safety and security.

Learning Activities:

1. Individually, observe and make notes of when we say or do something that seems to prompt defensiveness or conflict from the other. Set personal goals for reducing these behaviors. Then practice, observe, and adjust as needed.

2. Consult and agree on several communication practices we commit to using consistently. We can begin to compile the list now and then keep adding to it over a few weeks. Once we have a completed list, we can create a visual reminder to post in our home, on an electronic device, or both.

3. Obtain two large pieces of paper, one each, and a selection of various colored markers. For an agreed amount of time, use the markers on the paper to express our positive and negative feelings about a topic. The result can be anything from vigorous squiggles or slashes to something artistic. Share our "drawings" and talk about what was going through our minds.

4. Search the internet for and watch videos of Dr. John Gottman and others speaking about the couples' research at the Gottman Institute.

5. To increase our skill in using kind words, we will attempt what researcher Shaunti Feldhahn has developed called a "30-Day Kindness Challenge" (www.shaunti.com). This will assist us to see how kind words and actions transform a relationship. The Challenge has three aspects noted below.

1. "Say nothing negative about your person, either to them or about them to someone else."
2. "Every day, find one positive thing that you can sincerely praise or affirm about your person and tell them, and tell someone else."
3. "Every day, do a small act of kindness or generosity for your person."

Feldhahn says that when these three aspects come together, they react and build "something remarkable, beautiful, powerful, and, above all, transformative."[48] Shaunti Feldhahn

Couple Reflection and Consultation:

Throughout this couple guide, there are invitations to practice the Character Quality of Reflection about your interactions and connection. This practice gives you opportunities to celebrate progress and consult to address issues.

1. What makes it easier for us to begin interactions and conversations gently and kindly? (Consider preparation, looking after well-being, conscious awareness, practice…)
2. What benefits are there and how do we tend to respond to each other when an interaction starts with gentleness and kindness?
3. What is the outcome for us when we begin an interaction harshly or with criticism?
4. What helps us recover and re-balance to being unified partners after we have had a difficult interaction? What aids us with remembering to speak and act differently another time?

5. What would assist us with distinguishing between a complaint and a criticism? How can we respond to complaints constructively?
6. What specific actions will we take, or what personal growth efforts will we make, to improve our communications?
7. What are some areas that we want to reassess about our communication in the future? When will we reflect and consult about this?

Section 4:

Creating Connecting Experiences

Section 4 Introduction

Your connection as a couple is growing and becoming stronger. This section will now guide you through investing your time in more unity-building activities that increase vitality. As you laugh, play, and have good quality connecting time most days, you will move closer to feeling "as one".

Thoughtfulness for each other's well-being and happiness leads you to generously practice Service with one another. Mutually applying Service increases couple vitality.

The four Vitalizers in this section will weave together your bodies, minds, hearts, and souls.

In Section 4, you will learn about and apply:

- Vitalizer 10: Choosing to Merge
- Vitalizer 11: Enjoying Social Time
- Vitalizer 12: Sharing Laughter and Humor
- Vitalizer 13: Giving Thoughtful Service

Vitalizer 10: Choosing to Merge

"A tendency to turn toward your partner is the basis of trust, emotional connection, passion, and a satisfying sex life."
John M. Gottman and Nan Silver

Focus Statement: We respond positively to one another's requests to share time, and we choose to initiate, increase, and maintain our connection with one another and merge our lives.

Deeper Learning:

As we share experiences and live with each other, we develop patterns and habits that create a culture of how we respond to and connect. We look for opportunities to reach out to each other and create positive interactions. Our goal is oneness, where we achieve a union of our minds, hearts, bodies, and souls. Merging two lives is not easy, and at times it's difficult and painful. Our commitment to staying connected helps us apply Perseverance throughout this merging process.

Being a couple provides companionship for us. We protect and enhance our relationship when we pay attention and respond positively to each other's small and more significant requests to share moments and experiences. Dr. John Gottman, who researches couples, has observed that couples connect and attune to one another when they turn toward each other, which builds confidence and goodwill. These couples make minor and major "bids" for "each other's attention, affection, humor, or support." He indicates, "A tendency to turn toward your partner is the basis of trust, emotional connection, passion, and a satisfying sex life." Responding well to each other's "bids" then strengthens our connection.[49] John M. Gottman and Nan Silver

Often a request for connection from us can be somewhat indirect. We simply reach out to the other to draw notice to something or to share an interesting piece of information, tell a humorous story, or recount an experience we have just had. If our partner is engaged in an activity or distracted and working on their phone, tablet, or computer, our response can be minimal.

When we do not respond as we reach out to each other, we discourage connection, and we may cause hurt feelings. When we do respond and engage with each other, connection builds, and we have an opportunity to merge our attention toward something together. We may benefit from having our devices less present in some parts of our home, so we do not miss each other's bids to connect. Sometimes we can also prompt the busy partner to look up, become present, and connect. The goal is to increase our feelings of being unified partners through having a shared experience.

A Couple Shares Their Experience: *"My partner initially resisted learning about emotional bids for time. After I became upset, they ended up reading the material and making a conscious effort to engage with me differently. They offered words of appreciation every day. They also tried to listen for the feelings and emotions in the information I relayed, instead of just responding to the details. Now when I share about my work, they ask follow-up questions about how I am feeling or how my co-workers are feeling. Sometimes they also offer support and sympathy, like saying, 'Wow! That sounds tough.'*

"Now that a few weeks have passed, we are at a different place in our relationship and feel more connected. Today I asked how it felt to offer emotional support using words, as I knew it was an effort and was sometimes uncomfortable. They said it felt like using new muscles and that some attempts felt like a wobble, trip, and fall. For me, it has also been a new

experience—mostly positive—but I struggle at times with questions seeming intrusive. I need to remind myself to have patience, and that with continued practice, we will find a better balance in this phase of our lives."

With practice and careful observation, thoughtfulness toward each other can grow our connection. Attuning to each other can prompt us to notice when the other will likely have a difficult day and do what is needed for support. We can notice when something the other will enjoy is becoming available. We can pick up a special gift or offer a delicious meal. The goal is to be thoughtfully aware of what opportunities for connection we will each appreciate.

One practice in a couple relationship that builds a strong connection is how we respond to good news from each other, no matter how small or large:

> "Research shows that couples who regularly celebrate the good times have higher levels of commitment, intimacy, trust, and relationship satisfaction."[50] Tara Parker-Pope

Ways to respond could include enthusiasm, genuine interest, questions, expressions of pride or appreciation, hugs, a gift, a special meal, and time together.

Dr. William Doherty says intentional connection "rituals" are social interactions that are repeated, coordinated, and significant. Actions do not count as a "ritual" if they do not significantly contribute to our closeness. We can consider such rituals as how we greet one another, stay in communication throughout the day, or engage in an activity together. Perhaps we take a walk together once a week, watch a media program together, or cuddle at the end of each day. Consider as well whether we treat special anniversaries as occasions to observe and celebrate.[51]

Doherty says:

"What Leah [his wife] and I do during our talk ritual is an emotional check-in. It's 'How are you doing?' 'What has your day been like?' It's just a check-in. No problem solving, no logistics—just being friends savoring a brief interlude of personal conversation every day of their married lives."[52] William Doherty

Dr. Rob Skuka says there are three vital couple rituals: talking together a minimum of 15 to 20 minutes each day, and if possible, including partner appreciation sharing; having a weekly in-depth dialogue for at least 30-60 minutes to focus on a significant issue, problem, or way to enhance the relationship; and having fun together.[53]

A Couple Shares Their Experience: *"My partner always makes coffee, tells me they love me when leaving for work, and kisses me even if we have disagreed the night before. An argument is a pothole in our marriage; it's not the whole journey. So, for us, the rituals are symbols that we are in this for the long haul, not just for the time an argument takes."*

When we spend couple time together away from our responsibilities, such as on a date or a vacation, we can focus on enhancing our friendship. This can include checking in with what is happening in each other's lives and any emotional responses to situations we have going on. This check-in provides an opportunity to listen and be understanding and supportive.

Dr. Doherty provides some guidelines for this check-in time together:

- There needs to be a clear transition into the time together and a clear exit
- If the activity involves a conversation, avoid logistics talk (who did or will do what, where, or when)
- Avoid problem-fixing talk
- Avoid conflict[54]

[More about going on dates as a couple is in "Vitalizer 11: Enjoying Social Time".]

A Couple Shares Their Experience: *"We have developed a consistent practice in our marriage of checking in with each other for periodic updates. These maintain our close connection with one another. We can assess our progress and direction on decisions we have made related to a project, activity, or issue. We gain an understanding of each other's thoughts, feelings, desires, and beliefs when we ask open-ended questions in an encouraging and respectful tone of voice. Some examples of questions we use are:*

- *'How are you doing?'*
- *'How did your day go?'*
- *'How can I be supportive?'*
- *'What do you see are the next steps of our project?'*
- *'What unexpected demands are pressing on you that are important for me to know?'*
- *'What do you need from me, if anything, at this point?'*
- *'It will be a big day ahead for you. How do you feel?'*

"Consistent validations of Character Qualities, a mindful presence, thoughtful observation, and prompt sharing keep us

emotionally and spiritually connected. We make better decisions and avoid disunity. We are tuned into the pace and significant aspects of each other's lives as friends. This has been especially important for us when parenting young children and when we are doing home renovation projects."

Checking in with each other may be in person, but we also include text messages and calls, especially as we are transitioning from one activity or place to another. As we greet and leave one another, our communications are also often in the form of a loving smile, hug, or kiss—or all three!

Opportunities for couple merging and building a feeling of oneness happen daily. However, it can take time and repetition until a practice feels comfortable and something that we want to keep in our lives long-term. We start with a small number and build up our practices until they are part of the culture of our relationship.

Examples:

- Invite to watch a sunrise, sunset, rainbow, or stars.
- Share an article or something of interest.
- Request a listening ear or hug.
- Have a hug, kiss, or touch before parting; greet after being apart.
- Send a text message and/or photo of what we are doing.
- Make our bed with fresh sheets together.

Applying Character Qualities:

Below are some practical ways to incorporate character into daily practices with the theme of this chapter.

Creativity

- Initiate new ways to stay in close connection with each other.
- Take an action that we have used to connect us and make a change to it.
- Play a game or engage in a fun activity that deepens our knowledge of each other.

Dependability

- Respond consistently and positively to each other's bids for connection.
- Work promptly, proactively, and diligently on high-priority issues.
- Seek help from and rely on one another.

Orderliness

- Create repeatable and routine habits that support us in consulting about important issues relevant to our relationship.
- Plan a longer amount of time together to allow for a deeper connection.
- Notice when an action has the possibility of being a regular connection practice and systematically carry it out.

Learning Activity:

1. Determine the "rituals" or practices that we enjoy and that bring feelings of connection after we have been apart and begin to use them more regularly. Examples: hug, kiss, a few minutes sitting talking...

2. Plan a regular time for us to talk each day or week while enjoying coffee, tea, a snack, or a meal.

3. Plan a celebration of a current accomplishment one of us has had.

4. For an agreed amount of time, such as a week, carefully observe and respond to each other's bids for attention and connection. If a partner does not notice an outreach, do a gentle reminder. At the end of the time, consult about the effect on our relationship. Agree on what actions to continue.

5. Put music on we both enjoy and dance together in the house. Alternatively, we may enjoy music and dance in another location, even take dancing lessons together.

6. Consult about the concept of oneness and merging to be one unit as a couple. How can we achieve this feeling and level of functioning and still feel like we are unique individuals? What are the advantages to us of being merged into one?

Couple Reflection and Consultation:

Throughout this couple guide, there are invitations to practice the Character Quality of Reflection about your interactions and connection. This practice gives you opportunities to celebrate progress and consult to address issues.

1. What is our general attitude about emotional bids for attention? How do we generally respond to them?
2. When have we responded well to a bid for attention and connection?

3. When, if ever, does it feel like a problem or a burden to respond to each other's outreach in this way?
4. What do we celebrate in our lives? How do we celebrate?
5. What are some of our favorite couple connection "rituals" or practices?
6. How do we feel when we consistently connect through a couple "ritual"?
7. What connection practices do we want to increase, strengthen, or add?
8. When do we feel some resentment about what our partner invites us to do with them? What new approaches will we take so that resentment lessens?
9. What are our views about concepts like "merging" and "oneness"?

Vitalizer 11: Enjoying Social Time

"Great dates involve communicating with one another, reviving the spark that initially ignited your fire, and developing mutual interests and goals...."
Claudia and David Arp

Focus Statement: We enjoy deepening our friendship and connection with fun and relaxing social experiences by ourselves and with others.

Deeper Learning:

Many relationship and marriage experts advise having dates with each other at all stages of life and experience. They encourage us to do this no matter what our financial or family circumstances are. Sometimes our dates are inexpensive and simply time together when we can talk intimately. However, sometimes we choose to spend time and money to plan and carry out connection activities, as we see it's a worthwhile investment. It's even possible for us to have a couple date at home once the children are asleep, but this is not ideal as our children can wake up and interrupt us. This quotation is from one of our favorite experts on dates:

> "We believe that having a healthy, growing marriage relationship requires friendship, fun, and romance. And there's no better way to encourage all of these things than having dates! Great dates are more than going to see a movie and tuning out the world for a while. Great dates involve communicating with one another, reviving the spark that initially ignited your fire, and developing mutual interests and goals that are not focused on your careers or

> your children. Great dates can revitalize your relationship."[55] Claudia and David Arp

Science agrees that couple activities can assist us to stay current with each other's lives, help us be more supportive of each other, and reduce the chances of us ending our relationship. Dates are times when conversations and activities we both enjoy connect us emotionally. Keeping the dates interesting also contributes to connection and stress relief:

> "... [A] growing body of research suggests that couples who engage in novel activities that are fun and active, as opposed to the old standby of dinner and a movie, foster an even higher quality of balanced levels of closeness—as long as they choose activities that represent a shared interest of each partner's desires."[56] Les and Leslie Parrott and David H. Olson

A Couple Shares Their Experience: *"We found that every date we had was just going to dinner at the same places, and that was getting boring. Now we do Alphabet Dates each week, where we take turns and create a date that begins with a specific letter. It's fun and a surprise for the other person. Last week I had the letter "B", and we had Breakfast for dinner, a Bed made of Blankets on the Beach, and took Books along with us to read. It's fun to spend the week thinking about what to come up with for the letter and have that to look forward to. We also appreciate that we share taking the lead on the planning. Then, we share afterward what we enjoyed about the time together."*

We can show our commitment to couple time when we set aside some money for activities we enjoy. It can be tempting to focus only on sacrificing for our children and handling our financial responsibilities rather than also prioritizing our time together. Balance is needed, and it assists us when we remember that the well-being of our home and family is founded on our well-being as a couple.

Time together can include a variety of options, such as:

- Having a meal in a restaurant or picnic
- Talking on the phone or by video while one is away from home
- A spiritual gathering
- Exercising at the same time, such as going for a walk
- Doing a home maintenance project
- Watching a show or movie
- Attending a concert
- Playing a sport
- Engaging in sexual intimacy
- Going on a trip or vacation

We simply agree on our purpose for the activity and ensure that we include conversations that connect us and move our relationship forward.

A Couple Shares Their Experience: *"My partner enjoys going out to eat, so we do it sometimes when they suggest it. However, I am beginning to realize that I have not been appreciating this time as a type of romantic interlude, as well as a place to eat dinner. Now I am striving to improve our conversations when we go out, with fewer logistics and more relationship building."*

If we do activities together and end up feeling more distant, we reflect and review what happened and why we feel this way. We then consult and agree on what to do differently the next time. It's also wise to minimize our social media use and screentime while doing an activity together, so we ensure we are not interfering with our couple connection. If we notice increased screentime happening in our lives in general, we reflect and consult about why. Sometimes we may be avoiding each other, or there are underlying issues to address.

It can also connect us when we have social time offering hospitality or spending time with friends who are couples, but this is not the same as having our own couple time. The Character Quality of Moderation applies, so we also ensure we have time together on our own. [See more on involving others in "Vitalizer 19: Connecting with Friends and Community".]

Examples:

- Learning: museums, taking a course together
- Nature: boating, hiking, walking
- Exercise: swimming, biking
- Culture: concert, dancing
- Friends: picnic, shopping, sports

Applying Character Qualities:

Below are some practical ways to incorporate character into daily practices with the theme of this chapter.

Friendliness

- Include sharing of stories about our lives as part of our social experiences.
- Invite others to our home to have positive experiences together.
- Build relationships with other couples, so we can share social time with them.

Orderliness

- Make the plans and arrangements for regular couple activities.
- Gather and organize the necessary resources for activities.
- Agree on boundaries for topics to raise or not consult about during couple social activities.

Positive Spirit

- Express enthusiasm for each other's ideas and plans for social activities.
- Sincerely enjoy spending time together socially.
- Share positive appreciation for each other when carrying out or completing a social activity.

Learning Activities:

1. Create and enjoy two Alphabet Dates, one planned by each partner. [See the story in the chapter about these.]

2. Cooperatively plan a series of couple dates that include ones that happen at home and others that are out doing activities. Consider additional ones that we each plan separately as a surprise to the other, if we enjoy surprises. Consider what would have us be more relaxed about a surprise plan.

3. Plan and carry out a short (1-4 days) or long (5 days or more) vacation that will include rest, relaxation, and social experiences together.

Couple Reflection and Consultation:

Throughout this couple guide, there are invitations to practice the Character Quality of Reflection about your interactions and connection. This practice gives you opportunities to celebrate progress and consult to address issues.

1. How happy or unhappy are we with our amount of couple time? What do we want to improve?
2. What activities occur during our favorite dates?
3. Are we able to have fun and be playful with each other during social events? What types of activities make this more likely to occur?
4. Is learning something new or learning about each other something we value in social circumstances? What types of activities make this more likely to occur?
5. What stories do we have about couple-time adventures?
6. How do we manage the expenses of social time? Is there improvement we can carry out?
7. What arrangements for our children support us in relaxing and enjoying time when we are away from them?
8. What couple friendships do we have? What new outreach do we want to do? What types of activities would we enjoy together with them?
9. What is our attitude toward offering hospitality as a way of connecting us? What actions could we take to have the experience be unifying for us and positive for our guests?
10. How often do we take days away from home for a vacation experience? Do we need to do this more often or for longer? What are our favorite ways of doing this type of activity?

Vitalizer 12: Sharing Laughter and Humor

"Humor is about shared experiences
and a feeling of belonging."
Susan Sparks

Focus Statement: We prompt each other to laugh, use humor to respond to some of our challenges or irritations, and enjoy fun activities that lighten our lives.

Deeper Learning:

It's great when we can lighten up and laugh together to smooth our communications and link us in unity. We recognize that there are many opportunities to be serious in our life, but we see no need to be sour-faced or perpetually solemn. Humor, happiness, and joy are part of a life of vitality.

Laughter is a choice, and it's an experience that begins when we are babies. Sometimes as adults, however, we just lose track of what brings us joy. Sometimes we think we are too grown up to be silly and playful at times. Maybe it's time for us to lighten up a little.

> "We view marriage [and relationships] as a commitment between two people to love, honor, cherish, and *entertain* each other.... ... You owe your partner a great deal of laughter...it's a mutual obligation. ... You didn't commit to one another in order to annoy and make each other miserable. Rather, you joined together because you hoped to make each other happier. ... [W]e are not suggesting that you constantly keep each other in stitches. The serious and the routine are a part of all our lives. But these need to be punctuated with times of laughter."[57]
> Jeanette C. Lauer and Robert H. Lauer

It can increase our couple vitality when we are playful and humorous with each other at appropriate times. This is also true when we spend time together relaxing and enjoying an activity or date. When we build connection in these ways, we more easily respond to whatever is going on in our lives. [See "Vitalizer 11: Enjoying Social Time".]

Genuine humor generates positive feelings and happiness throughout our life. One way we prompt laughter and experience vitality is to tell stories about our experiences. As we bring laughter to each other, it raises our happiness. We are then more likely to laugh with others.

One challenge with humor is that we can misuse it. For example, if we pair laughter with sarcasm, ridicule, tromping on feelings, personal put-downs, or prejudice, we cause harm rather than produce joy and love. However, humor can take the form of gentle teasing as a way to accept each other's foibles or unique approaches to tasks. This lighter approach can prevent us from reacting with criticism or conflict.

Sometimes we attempt humor, but it does not work as well as we want. Each person finds different things funny at times. One of us may laugh, and the other is baffled and does not get a joke at all. Sometimes we may use humor as a shield to avoid revealing our true feelings. The other person may then miss our point or not take it seriously. It takes courage to be more direct and not hide behind a laugh.

A Couple Shares Their Experience: *"When we began living together, every time I left the room briefly, my partner would turn the light off. I would go back into the room in darkness, which was very annoying. I realized this strong need to conserve electricity could be a source of regular conflict. Instead, we became playful about it. Sometimes I turn the light off when my partner is still in a room. I tease them about whether they are getting anxious when they leave a light on* *unnecessarily. We joke about whether we can see in the dark. We now own amazing flashlights. Being 'light' about this has become an unexpected source of fun."*

Below are some insights about laughter, joy, and spirituality:

> "Laughter is a spiritual practice. ... The transformative nature of any spiritual discipline comes with regular practice. When done consistently, it can eventually change our lives. If we make time to invite joy into our lives each day, we will become more aware of joy and laughter in our lives and in the world. Eventually, laughter will become an innate part of who we are."[58] Susan Sparks

> "Cultivate humor as a higher path—a cosmic contentment that is truly lighthearted and full of joy. You will lighten the lives of others simply by the radiance of your good humor. Even the briefest laugh reminds us that we have available a kind of spiritual gold anytime, anywhere."[59] Stephen Post

A Couple Shares Their Experience: *"Laughter is healing medicine for the soul, mind, and heart. Laughter melts away imagined differences and brings to the forefront that we are all related in a very real way. It unites us. Joy for me is about detachment from the changes and chances of this world. Joy is a kindness to us and others. When I am experiencing joy, I have more energy, I find life more pleasing and funnier in general. I am better able to show compassion and empathize with others. I can serve others with grace and cheerfulness. I find it easier to think of others' needs and forget my selfish wants. Others are happier around me when I am happy and joyful!"*

The ability to laugh together and appreciate the humorous aspects of our lives can strengthen our relationship and family life. As one of us shares a story, laughter can spread to lift the spirits of the other and out to family members and friends.

> "It is a rare and beautiful quality to feel truly happy when others are happy. When someone rejoices in our happiness, we are flooded with respect and gratitude for their appreciation. When we take delight in the happiness of another, when we genuinely rejoice at their prosperity, success, or good fortune rather than begrudging it in any way, we are abiding in … sympathetic joy…."[60]
> Sharon Salzberg

> "Humor is about shared experiences and a feeling of belonging. It improves our mood through social connections. And when we feel less alone, we feel stronger."[61] Susan Sparks

Connecting through laughter, humor, and social time as a couple can:

- Increase the strength of our friendship
- Make it easier to cope with workload and difficulties
- Encourage and assist us and each other with personal growth and improvement
- Increase energy and productivity
- Deepen our emotional and physical intimacy
- Increase harmony and couple satisfaction
- Add balance to our busy lives
- Prompt us to relax and not take ourselves too seriously
- Remind us to feel grateful for our lives, each other, and family
- Assist us with building friendships with others

A Couple Shares Their Experience: *"One of the elements of our couple vision was to have a fun social time at least every few weeks. We kept struggling to carry it out, focusing instead on all the serious parts of our life. One day we saw some research about the importance of couple connection, and so we decided to get serious about having fun! We set up a folder and began saving money in it. When there was enough for an activity, we made specific plans and carried them out. We discovered that we liked spending time together this way!"* [See "Vitalizer 3: Where Are We Going?" about visioning.]

Our ability to enjoy being with each other, no matter what the circumstances are, is a strong power in keeping us connected.

Examples:

- Watch a comedy show, play, or movie
- Gently tease each other about something silly
- Share a funny story from an experience
- Create a couple date that maximizes laughter

Applying Character Qualities:

Below are some practical ways to incorporate character into daily practices with the theme of this chapter.

Creativity

- Consciously look for new ways to prompt laughter between us.
- Develop a new method of assisting each other to relax.
- Share stories regularly.

Moderation

- Know when to be humorous and when to be serious.
- Balance our life with regular humor.
- Laugh *with* each other, not *at* each other.

Positive Spirit

- Maintain positivity, optimism, and enthusiasm even when things become difficult.
- Use humor in ways that uplift each other and diffuse tension.
- Rise above immediate emotional distress, or annoyance at each other's quirks, keeping in mind the long-term happiness in the relationship.

Learning Activities:

1. **Building Storytelling Skills:** One of us shares a story, pausing every few sentences to allow the listener to ask a question or make a summarizing statement that checks for understanding. Take time to clarify if we do not seem to be completely understanding each other. At the end of the story, the listener summarizes and shares:

    a. What seemed important from the experience the speaker had.
    b. What feelings they heard the speaker experience (Examples: anger, sadness, happiness, frustration, excitement...).
    c. How they felt while listening to the story: What was the effect of this story on them? What moved, touched, or inspired them?
    d. Were there any humorous aspects to the story that they enjoyed?

2. **Building Sharing Humor Skills:** The action components below can be carried out just with each other or with others involved. After each story or joke, the listeners share what was funny (or not) to them, how they responded to the humor, and what they learned.

    a. Funny stories about the relationships or marriages of our parents, grandparents, other relatives, or friends.
    b. Funny stories about our couple relationship or family life.
    c. Funny stories from a recent (or childhood) experience.
    d. Jokes or puns.

3. Consult about an interaction we have repeatedly about something that annoys us but is not likely to change, and then determine a way to respond with humor and playfulness instead.

4. Find and share a video, movie, or comedy show to learn what we each find funny. If one of us does not find the item funny, search to find material that we both respond to with laughter.

Couple Reflection and Consultation:

Throughout this couple guide, there are invitations to practice the Character Quality of Reflection about your interactions and connection. This practice gives you opportunities to celebrate progress and consult to address issues.

1. How do we feel when we laugh? What often makes each of us laugh?
2. Are we able to tell stories to each other? What would remind us to do this activity more often?

3. Do we joke or tease in a way that seems to uplift each other?
4. What prompts us to be fun and playful with each other? How does this benefit our connection?
5. When have laughter and humor increased our connection with one another? Increased our connection to others?
6. When has humor made us feel more distant from one another? Do we ever use humor in a way that may be hurtful, such as speaking with sarcasm or poking at sensitive areas? What would help us form new behaviors?
7. How do we respond to physical humor? To intellectual humor?
8. What activities might prompt us to laugh more and feel more connected?

Vitalizer 13: Giving Thoughtful Service

"Requests are a means to develop
the kind of partnership that takes into account
each other's needs, wants, and desires."
Sandra Gray Bender

Focus Statement: We communicate about our wishes and needs and apply Service to fulfill them for each other.

Deeper Learning:

Over time and with mutual communication and encouragement, we build awareness of what words and actions we can offer that benefit each other. With practice, we increasingly fulfill each other's needs by offering our Service. When we receive this offering from each other, it feels like receiving love, and we express sincere appreciation.

While it's great to anticipate each other's needs, we are often not capable of doing that. It's a mistake if we think that if our partner loves and cares about us, they should automatically know what we need. To sort all of this out and keep our relationship in balance, we must regularly consult with each other to determine what actions to take. We must also consult about what we can and cannot do and what others can do to help. We give each other the grace of words and make requests of each other, and then we do our best to show Compassion and be thoughtful and considerate in response. [See more about avoiding mind-reading in "Vitalizer 5: Understanding Each Other".]

> "... [O]ne aspect of the partnership is determining what each will do for the other. Requests are a means to develop

the kind of partnership that takes into account each other's needs, wants, and desires."[62] Sandra Gray Bender

As we both apply the Character Quality of Service within our relationship and family, we keep reciprocity in place. This prevents or eliminates destructive self-centered or selfish behavior patterns. Here is a perspective on this dynamic:

> "The antidote to selfishness is service. It is difficult to be selfish when you are serving your spouse. Service forces you to put the needs of your spouse in front of your own needs. One of the keys to a strong marriage lies in fulfilling your spouse's needs before your own. When you use this key, a spirit of service will soon permeate your relationship. This spirit of service is contagious."[63] "Marriage, Increase the Joy, Decrease the Misery"

When we serve each other, we create a general culture where both of us feel satisfied and cared about. Naturally, as individuals, we have personal needs that we must look after ourselves. However, when we can assist each other, it strengthens our Trust and increases our love for one another. For example, one of us might need time alone to recharge energy batteries, and our partner notices the fatigue level, encourages rest, and takes on some extra tasks.

A Couple Shares Their Experience: *"What I love in our relationship is that we each regularly practice service with each other in kind, courteous, and thoughtful ways. These actions smooth the rough corners of life and assist us with appreciating each other. Fixing a meal, holding a door open, setting the table, getting the mail, providing a glass of water, checking the functioning of a vehicle, bringing a small gift, massaging a* *neck, providing reminders, and more all help our relationship and home flow more smoothly and peacefully."*

However, we also know that busyness, distraction, health issues, and other limitations can sometimes make it difficult to see and fulfill each other's needs. When we do not share, recognize, or meet key expectations and needs, disunity and difficulties can result. Willard Harley observes in his work that people will often violate even their own most fundamental values to meet their perceived needs. Recognizing and meeting one another's needs is one of many ways to prevent the unhappiness, resentment, relationship breakdown, and infidelity that at times can result from consistently unmet needs. Harley says:

> "Often the failure of men and women to meet each other's emotional needs is simply due to ignorance of each other's needs and not selfish unwillingness to be considerate. Fulfilling those needs does not mean you have to painfully grit your teeth, making the best of something you hate. It means preparing yourself to meet needs you may not appreciate yourself. By learning to understand your spouse as a totally different person than you, you can begin to [meet] that person's emotional needs."[64]
> Willard F. Harley, Jr.

When we know each other's primary needs, we know what the high priorities for action are. Our union is likely to be stronger and happier when we meet these needs to the best of our ability. We apply Moderation, give thoughtful attention, and ensure that we are both actively engaged. As we feel our own needs are met, we feel stronger and more able to reach out and meet our partner's needs.

A Couple Shares Their Experience: *"For years my wife Keri and I struggled. … [O]ur personalities didn't quite match up. And the longer we were married the more extreme the differences seemed. … Our fighting became so constant that it was difficult to even imagine a peaceful relationship. We became perpetually defensive, building emotional fortresses around our hearts. We were on the edge of divorce and more than once we discussed it.*

"Through time I've learned that our experience was an illustration of a much larger lesson about marriage. The question everyone in a committed relationship should ask their significant other is, 'What can I do to make your life better?' … Real love is … to expand our own capabilities of tolerance and caring, to actively seek another's well-being. All else is simply a charade of self-interest."[65] *Richard Paul Evans*

We also benefit from identifying the needs we have as a couple that we want to create solutions for together. For example, these needs could include social time, hospitality, or sexual intimacy. Our focus is on addressing the elements that create a harmonious relationship and household. When this harmony exists, we can feel secure and more easily reach out to meet the needs of others.

Our needs will change as our union grows and matures. Significant events related to children, work, or our health also prompt us to review our needs. The intensity of our needs will often fluctuate as well. It's wise to re-examine our relationship periodically to be sure we are recognizing and meeting each other's most vital needs, as well as those that simply contribute to the quality of each other's life. The prioritization of our needs may also adjust with time and experiences as a couple. We can also establish a practice of simply asking the other what we can do to help them right then.

Some examples of practicing thoughtful Service to each other are:

- Offering and fixing something to drink or eat
- Washing clothes that the other needs for an activity or event
- Bringing a gift that uplifts the other through a difficult time
- Looking after the needs of young children so the other can rest
- Fixing something in the home that is a safety hazard
- Massaging a sore part of the body
- Listening carefully to what is shared

It's naturally challenging to meet each other's needs consistently. Life is full of adventures, and there are often disruptions in the flow between us due to work requirements, meeting the needs of children or family members, illness, and more. It's unreasonable and unrealistic to expect that any partner can meet all of one's needs and expectations all the time. We can do our best, but it's wise to avoid thinking that we are in serious trouble when we cannot be perfect at this. Using Reflection and consultation are vital, so we determine what works well for both of us. In this process, we consider:

- When sacrifice is an appropriate choice,
- When Moderation is needed, and
- When to apply Creativity to develop alternatives.

Here is a reflection on expectations:

> "In general, you will be disappointed or happy in life depending on how well your perceptions of what is happening match what you expected—what you think

should be happening. It's not surprising, therefore, that expectations play a crucial role in how happy your marriage will be. ... [I]t may not be as crucial for the two of you to hold all the same expectations as it is for each of you to do your best to try to meet the important (and realistic) desires of the other."[66] Howard J. Markman, Scott M. Stanley, and Susan L. Blumberg

As we grow as individuals, we learn when it's great to acknowledge or celebrate our practice of Service to each other and when it's fine if there is little or no response. The genuine practice of Service does not seek credit, because it's a gift to the recipient. We serve each other out of love and caring, not out of a wish to be noticed and praised.

A Couple Shares Their Experience: *"Practicing service within my family is all about everyone working together to set everyone else up for good outcomes. There are many little things that I do regularly for the express purpose of setting my partner up for success instead of failure and without making them feel belittled or micromanaged. Most services that I provide to my partner are completed without them ever realizing that I am doing them. There is usually no appreciation beyond my seeing the result, which is all that is usually necessary for me."*

Caution: Due to trauma or due to psychological or emotional problems, some partners may feel they do not deserve to have needs, communicate them, or have them met. In other cases, partners can adopt a selfish attitude of entitlement that their needs are most important. Yet others may blame themselves or others for unmet needs. Partners can contribute to healing these perceptions; however, some people may also need professional assistance.

Remember, too, that healthy individuals also have a responsibility to maintain their own well-being and happiness. While couples contribute to each other, the individual partners cannot expect someone else to "make" them healthy or happy. Most couples also discover that people other than a partner can meet some of their needs effectively, such as close friends. Remember that it's wise to agree about who outside of each other is meeting the needs, so there is no harm to the relationship.

Examples:

- Preparing a beverage or food for the other.
- Obtaining clothing for a special occasion.
- Consulting about a work problem.
- Providing energy recharge time and space.
- Saying a prayer for each other.
- Buying groceries.
- Planning a trip and making reservations.

Applying Character Qualities:

Below are some practical ways to incorporate character into daily practices with the theme of this chapter.

Friendliness

- Respond to each other's requests and needs with warmth and generosity.
- Make ourselves available to listen, share, encourage, and accompany each other through whatever arises.
- Develop shared interests and activities.

Humility

- Stop our activities to focus on each other's wishes or needs.
- Acknowledge how valuable our partner's well-being is to the relationship.
- Respond willingly and positively to requests for our attention or help.

Service

- Notice and thoughtfully consider what to give to and receive from each other and carry out the best actions possible.
- Listen attentively and try to determine what each person is truly communicating and needing.
- Confidently initiate positive action, believing that loving actions can contribute significantly to the quality of our relationship.

Learning Activities:

1. Reflect together on our primary needs and how they can be met using the list below, which is in no order. Choose the top three that are most important to each of us. Consider such items as:

    - Affection, Connection, and Love
    - Admiration and Significance*
    - Sexual Fulfillment
    - Financial Income and Management
    - Conversation
    - Recreational Companionship
    - Spiritual Companionship
    - Partnership
    - Resolution

- Openness
- Attractiveness
- Domestic Support
- Marriage/Partner Commitment
- Spontaneity and Variety
- Family Commitment
- Certainty and Security
- Personal Growth
- Humor, Laughter, and Lightness
- Being of Service[67]

* "Admiration and Significance" is defined as: "Respects, values, and appreciates me, helping me feel special and unique as a person and as a partner; makes negative comments only rarely and then with kindness; acknowledges my accomplishments; expresses admiration to me clearly and often."
Susanne M. Alexander

2. Consult and identify two new ways we can demonstrate Service to each other. Carry them out and reflect on the outcome.

Couple Reflection and Consultation:

Throughout this couple guide, there are invitations to practice the Character Quality of Reflection about your interactions and connection. This practice gives you opportunities to celebrate progress and consult to address issues.

1. What are our beliefs and attitudes about demonstrating Service to each other?

2. In what ways do we show that meeting each other's needs is important to us?
3. What areas in our lives may have become unbalanced, with one of us doing much more for the other, our, family, and around our home than the other? What will we adjust in this situation?
4. How do we address situations in which our needs are not being met as well as we want?
5. How could we handle a situation where one of us strongly insists that the other carry out actions to benefit us that they are unwilling or unable to do?
6. If we do not show a positive attitude when serving each other, how do we feel about the actions we receive?
7. What needs could we thoughtfully meet for each other that we are not currently doing?
8. Are we doing any actions that we believe demonstrate Service, but they are unwise as they handicap the other's ability to take responsibility?
9. How does our example of demonstrating Service to each other provide a model to others, such as our children or friends?

Section 5:

Forging Deeper Connection

Section 5 Introduction

As you navigate more sensitive topics, and as you learn and grow your unity together through challenges, you forge a deeper connection with one another.

Sexual intimacy is a key area of union for a couple. However, being able to talk about what you appreciate and your skillfulness in working through challenges with sex demonstrate your maturity and strength.

Money is another area that your personal experiences and attitudes affect. Couple vitality builds as you understand each other's viewpoints, consult, and come to unified agreements on how to manage money.

Throughout your life together, there will always be challenges to understand and conquer, new skills to learn, and forgiveness to practice. You will grow and develop as individuals and as a couple. Opportunities will arise to reclaim unity when it slips and resiliently rebound from difficult times.

In Section 5 you will dive deeper into:

- Vitalizer 14: Communicating About Sex
- Vitalizer 15: Managing Our Money
- Vitalizer 16: Growing from Difficulties
- Vitalizer 17: Resolving and Rebounding

Vitalizer 14: Communicating About Sex

"Emotional connection creates great sex,
and great sex creates deeper emotional connection."
Sue Johnson

Focus Statement: We value our physical intimacy that happens in the context of our emotional intimacy and love, and we share thoughts and feelings about our sex life to build deeper understanding, determine new actions, and strengthen our connection.

Deeper Learning:

We create our sexual and sensual experiences together. It builds our connection when we share what types of touch and experiences we value, and which ones are best to adjust or change. This mutual dynamic of sharing can enhance experiences for both of us and create increased oneness.

Our experiences and the responsiveness of our bodies will vary over time and in changing circumstances. However, our ability to consult through any challenges that arise will enhance our ability to keep physical touch as a key element that unites us. Here are some insights:

> "There are two key factors related to satisfying sex: emotional connection and conversations about sex. The second one often gets overlooked, but research shows that only 9% of couples who can't talk comfortably about sex report sexual satisfaction. By talking about sex, couples develop a 'script' or 'playbook' for how to please one another emotionally and sexually. ... That's why it's vital for couples to not only prioritize sex in the relationship, but also to learn how to talk about sex comfortably on a

> consistent basis. How can you make it more comfortable? Sharing your likes and dislikes about sex isn't a difficult task in itself, but being that vulnerable (even with your soulmate!) can make it a very difficult task. To make it more comfortable, try to think about sex as a physical expression of your friendship. At its core, the goal of sex is to become closer friends and have fun together. This reframing makes it a friendship issue, which is easier to address than a sexual issue."[68] Get Lasting

The link between sex and emotional connection is important:

> "... [S]ecure bonding and fully satisfying sexuality go hand in hand; they cue off and enhance each other. Emotional connection creates great sex, and great sex creates deeper emotional connection. When partners are emotionally accessible, responsive, and engaged, sex becomes intimate play, a safe adventure. Secure partners feel free and confident to surrender to sensation in each other's arms, explore and fulfill their sexual needs, and share their deepest joys, longings, and vulnerabilities. Then, lovemaking is truly making love."[69] Sue Johnson

Our ability to share honestly and listen lovingly with each other about such a personal topic can lead to enhanced experiences between us. [You have been learning about meeting each other's needs throughout this book, including in "Vitalizer 7: Loving One Another" and in "Vitalizer 13: Giving Thoughtful Service".]

Success Factors

There is a time and place for everything, including consultations about sex and touch. These are usually best if we are in a private place where we will not be interrupted, and we can truly hear what is on each other's minds. We have learned that it's best for us to be gently honest:

> "Discussions about sexual issues should come from a place of love and from a wish for maximizing the sexual experience for both of you. When you bring up the subject, here are a few tips to get what you want out of the discussion:
>
> - Be direct...
> - Use humor...
> - Start with a positive...."[70] Scott Haltzman

While we are often comfortable talking about our sexual intimacy, sometimes it does become difficult. We must stay aware of how our words affect each other. We are often very sensitive about topics related to our bodies and how they function as well as our preferences related to touch. It's essential that our consultations are affirming, encouraging, and loving.

Compassion is a great Character Quality for us to apply when we raise something about the other person and what they are doing or not doing. As we share about our own bodies and emotions and raise our concerns, we can then see the situation from our partner's perspective. We accompany each other, and we do our best to be careful with difficult requests and enthusiastic with fun suggestions we both appreciate.

A Couple Shares Their Experience: *"When we first became a serious couple, we talked about our sexual histories more than our preferences. This was important in helping us understand each other and our responses. Now we tend to focus more on our preferences.*

"Over the years of experiencing touch, learning what is sensitive to each of us, and observing responses to different experiences, we can usually sense when there is something to talk about. We have learned not to initiate consultations in the middle of experiences, as that seems to derail our involvement and arousal. Later, we can talk about what went well, what we would have preferred, and what is something new to try.

"On such a sensitive topic, we are careful to avoid any words that seem critical or that might prompt the other to feel insecure or devalued. We are careful to affirm to each other that our intimate experiences are something we value, and we are consulting about them to enhance our experiences."

We have noticed that sometimes we cannot immediately respond to what each other raises, because it's such a personal topic. At times we have an emotional reaction, and it takes a few hours or days to be clear about what we are thinking and feeling. This delay may be especially true if the topic reminds us of difficult experiences in the past. It's helpful to notice and share when something that happened previously is affecting us in the present.

Enhancing Experiences with Character

Our character strengths influence the quality of our consultations about sex. They also influence the quality of our sensual and sexual experiences. Character Qualities such as Flexibility, Respect, Creativity, and Trust assist us to explore and learn each other's sensual and sexual preferences. These Qualities also contribute to our connection:

> "A spiritual relationship is the radiant result of mutually expressed compassion. The connection happens on all levels—emotional, intellectual, sensual, and sexual. It's a powerful resonance that emanates from one soul's recognition of another. This is the best kind of relationship, and it engenders the absolute best kind of sex. When you have this kind of union, intercourse becomes much more than physical pleasure. It's alive with waves of appreciation and bone-tingling love. When the joy is centered in the heart—not just in the genitals—there's nothing else like it!"[71] Sandra Anne Taylor

A Couple Shares Their Experience: *"Touching each other deeply fulfills our need for love and caring. Often, we blend our physical, emotional, and spiritual feelings toward each other. We view sexual intimacy as a way to joyfully connect."*

Character Qualities that assist us in being intimate include Adherence and Dependability, which are vital components of the "attachment circuitry" that supports commitment and faithfulness to one another:

> "… [T]he first condition for a healthy and truly satisfying sexual connection is a commitment, with absolute faithfulness, to a relationship that will endure…. [I]t is the attachment circuitry, which comes into play in the long-term commitment of a couple to each other, that brings the greatest amount of sexual satisfaction."[72]
> Raymond and Furugh Switzer

Physical Factors

Sexual functioning is biologically complex. When we are not certain about how our bodies function, we find it useful to learn from and consult with experts. We discovered this key insight in our reading:

> "... [F]or some people, sexual desire—the urge to become sexual—doesn't *precede* feeling aroused; it actually follows it. In other words, some people rarely (or never) find themselves fantasizing about sex or feeling sexual urges, but when they're open to becoming sexual with their spouses anyway, they often find the sexual stimulation pleasurable, and they become aroused. Once aroused, there is a desire to continue. And that's every bit as much 'sexual desire' as the more traditional view of things."[73] Michele Weiner Davis

We also see and understand that our bodies change regularly, including from fluctuating hormones, illness, injury, and aging, and this affects our sex life.

A Couple Shares Their Experience: *"As our bodies change throughout life, we notice a need for flexibility, humor, cooperation, and understanding. We also see how important it is to stay as physically fit as possible."*

Here are some further thoughts:

> "The major functions of marital sexuality are a shared pleasure, a means to deepen and strengthen intimacy, and a tension reducer to deal with the stresses of life and marriage. ... There are myriad ways of being sexual. ... Sometimes sex can be long, tender, warm, and involving

(like a four-course gourmet dinner). Other times sex can be short and lusty (like a hamburger and fries). Marital sex is a mix and match depending on your feelings, needs, and practical and time constraints. If all sex were 'quickies' or a 3-hour lovemaking experience, it would become boring. Sexuality can be intimate or playful, a late-night way to end the day or a middle-of-the-day main event, a way to reconnect after a conflict, or a pleasant reassurance. The essence of creative sexuality is awareness of your feelings and needs with freedom to communicate desires and share with your spouse.

"The prescription for satisfying marital sex is integrating emotional intimacy, nondemand pleasuring, and erotic scenarios and techniques. These will not be present at each experience but are the foundation for healthy marital sexuality."[74] Barry and Emily J. McCarthy

Caution: When sharing with each other about your couple sexual experiences, your goal is to practice Compassion. This assists you to listen, understand, and find new approaches that are acceptable for both of you to try. If you are frustrated in this process, you may need to seek assistance from an expert in the field, or through books, videos, or counseling.

You may also need to seek medical or counseling support if something is interfering with your experiences, such as pornography or fetishes, previous trauma, addictions, attraction to someone else, or physical or emotional impairment. Mid-life physical changes can raise challenges, such as vaginal dryness or erection issues. You may find it helpful to consult with professionals and try medications, supplements, or specific exercises.

Examples:

- "I find it difficult to breathe and relax when you are fully on top of me. I wonder what different positions we could try?"
- "It arouses me when you touch me in these ways and places: ____. Are you willing to try these?"
- "What could I do that would bring you greater pleasure?"
- "It does not concern me that a climax/orgasm didn't happen, but I do feel hurt that you turned away from me afterward. Could we please talk about this?"
- "Could we experiment with trying ____ next time?"
- "I am frustrated that we are having sex less often, and I am also concerned about why. Can you please share with me what seems to be happening?
- "Hearing the kids in the other room put the brakes on my arousal and response to you. What can we do to help me with this? Would intimacy with different timing be possible?"

Applying Character Qualities:

Below are some practical ways to incorporate character into daily practices with the theme of this chapter.

Compassion

- Understand the sensitive nature of each other's history with sexual experiences and touch.
- Observe and respond with lovingkindness when either of us has a challenge with performance or limitations.
- Approach a resumption of sensual or sexual activity after a time of necessary abstinence with advance consultation and with care and gentleness.

Trust

- Consult about sex carefully, demonstrating Respect for each other's sensitivities and challenges.
- Maintain faithfulness to one another in words and actions.
- Demonstrate confidence in each other's goodwill intentions and gestures of affection and touch.

Truthfulness

- Share what we each believe about what is happening and why.
- Avoid making assumptions and proceed with bravely raising requests and concerns, believing that there may be new options to try.
- Patiently communicate acceptance of circumstances and functioning that cannot be changed.

Learning Activities:

1. Go for a walk in an attractive area of nature, holding hands. Take turns talking generally about our sexual intimacy experiences together. Agree on one new different action to take, carry it out, and reflect on the experience together. ***Note:*** This arrangement may contribute to you feeling safely connected, and the reduced eye contact may make the conversation more comfortable.

2. Choose two or three Character Qualities to focus on regularly incorporating into our sexual experiences.

3. Experiment with different frequencies for sexual experiences and assess our responses to them. What are our preferences regarding frequency? How can we adjust when there are differences with this?

4. Consult about our timing for sexual intimacy:
   a. Are we being spontaneous? Planning for our time together? Doing a combination of both?
   b. What could help us be successful? (Examples: the location, nearness of other people, time of day, locks on doors...)

Couple Reflection and Consultation:

Throughout this couple guide, there are invitations to practice the Character Quality of Reflection about your interactions and connection. This practice gives you opportunities to celebrate progress and consult to address issues.

Note: These consultations may be difficult and emotional. You can pause after reading each question to use your Reflection individually and then begin to share, taking turns as appropriate. It's wise to carefully avoid assuming what each of you will say and stay open to fully listening. Take breaks as needed.

1. What makes it easier for us to talk about our sex life?
2. What do we consider as the primary purposes of sex? Of sensual touch?
3. When has sexual intimacy felt most unifying to us? How could we increase a feeling of oneness between us during physical and sexual intimacy?
4. What are our views about how our thoughts, emotions, and spiritual connection affect our sexual intimacy? What would increase our connection related to sex?
5. What type of negative interactions between us affect the frequency or quality of our sexual experiences? How do our stress levels affect our experiences?

6. What enhances our sexual pleasure? What interferes with it?
7. How or when is cleanliness important as a factor in our experiences? Do we need to increase cleanliness to enhance intimacy?
8. What do we most appreciate about each other's bodies and sexual actions and responses?
9. What prompts arousal in each of us? How can we assist each other to feel aroused? What causes arousal and involvement in the experience to slow down or stop?
10. What specific requests for experiences do we each have? Are we willing or able to try accommodating these? What would make it easier for us to relax about carrying them out?
11. What types of touch or experiences are we uncomfortable with or directly request not happen?
12. At times when sexual intimacy is not possible, but we still want to be touched, what types of touch do we prefer?
13. Would we benefit from learning more about how male and female anatomy and physiology work? What are good sources of accurate information? (Please consider *Come As You Are* by Emily Nagoski.)
14. Are there issues for us with infidelity through pornography or contact with someone else emotionally or in-person who is outside of our couple relationship? How are we addressing the situation? What more do we need to do?
15. Are there experiences from before our relationship that were negative or abusive that are affecting either of us now? How are we addressing these?
16. What indications are there that we need help from professional services, a support group, or both?

Vitalizer 15: Managing Our Money

"Taking the time to figure out what's really going on when there are money conflicts will make your relationship richer, more compassionate, and more successful."
Syble Solomon

Focus Statement: We look at money as a resource entrusted to us to manage well, and we strive to agree about how we and others responsibly manage our money—earning, saving, investing, and sharing it according to our values.

Deeper Learning:

As we consult about and manage our finances well, we see how money fits into our unified vision and connection efforts. We see money as a valuable resource, and we do our best to earn what is needed, spend and give responsibly, consider the well-being of all family members, and plan for our short and long-term future. [See "Vitalizer 3: Where Are We Going?" about visioning.]

Many couples struggle at times with topics related to money, and that includes us. Managing finances can be complex, and it's in grappling with that complexity that we grow and deepen our relationship. To protect our unity, we ensure that we consult about all decisions that involve our finances. We also keep both of us fully and regularly informed about the state of our finances and how to access our resources. We review our records and plans as needed when circumstances in our life change.

Caution: Be careful about how much you share financial and password information and decisions before you are in a seriously committed relationship or marriage.

Our History and Values

We have layers of emotional connections to money, and these often lead to power and control issues for how we manage and use it. The values we each hold related to earning an income, spending, saving, giving, investing, and managing money usually link to experiences in our homes growing up and in the years before being together as a couple. These values from earlier in life may contribute to couple harmony or be very divergent. The goal as a couple is to consult and agree on a shared set of values and practices that we each agree to abide by to the best of our ability.

There may also be history from early in our relationship when we were less skillful that still affects us today. Often our experiences and observations related to money both from our childhood and in our relationship cause us to act or react automatically to money experiences now.

When a disagreement arises between us, it's good to do fact-finding that includes a gentle inquiry about why the issue seems so emotionally charged. Syble Solomon, an expert with Money Habitudes (www.moneyhabitudes.com) on the psychology of money, suggests the following to couples:

> "Money is a complex topic and pushes more hot buttons than any other issue in a relationship. When money seems to be the cause of conflict, it's a good time to step back, take a deep breath, and give yourselves some space. This time-out will help you to discover what's really going on. ... Money represents power, control, freedom, success, security, acceptance, status, love, and many other strong emotional needs. These needs may be associated with memories that can be pleasant, hurtful, exciting, or scary. These needs and memories often cause you to react strongly to what seems to be a money issue in your

relationship. … Taking the time to figure out what's really going on when there are money conflicts will make your relationship richer, more compassionate, and more successful."[75]

A Couple Shares Their Experience: *"When we were dating, I wanted to make a big deal about Valentine's Day [a North American holiday that encourages expressions of affection], but my partner did not. I had gone many years as a single person without someone to share the day with. However, my partner had worked for a florist one Valentine's Day, and the materialism involved with spending money to express love truly bothered them. We had a sincere consultation about this, and we decided that we could both agree to exchange romantic cards. We do not purchase gifts, decorate, or make it a special day in the family with certain foods and gifts for the children. Our children receive Valentine's Day cards from grandparents and participate in exchanges of cards at school. We both treasure the cards we exchange, our children see our loving words, and we have not invested in the materialism that certain 'holidays' have become.*

"Because we realized that we had both come to our marriage with expectations, in the first few years we thought about how we wanted to celebrate special calendar days and what types of money we wanted to spend doing it. We decided that birthdays were the important day for each member of the family, such as special meals, gifts, a trip to a museum, or a movie. We decided that we would not exchange gifts on our wedding anniversary but instead, we would buy something for our home together, which we have enjoyed. Every five years we buy tickets to a play or opera we really want to see. This has brought us much pleasure. By consulting together early in our marriage about holiday expectations, we have been able to

craft a family culture that emphasizes events, activities, and expressions of caring rather than possessions."

Character and Choices

As we observe and consult about managing our money, we realize that our Character Qualities and our values affect our choices. When money is used in beneficial ways, it's a source of great good. We can practice generosity to others and practice responsibility in financial activities.

Choice and the use of Moderation are consistent themes as we consult about the topic of money. We can choose to be thrifty in managing our money, or we can spend lavishly. We consider charitable donations and how generously to give. When would giving a lot of money be harmful to our family's well-being, and we need to apply Moderation? We think about whether it's important to us to accumulate wealth and possessions. We assess whether we display competitive behavior, buying what we see others buying—the newest and best clothes, jewelry, videogame, vehicle, or home. What if we tried to keep up with this activity to the point we went into debt? Are we responsible for paying our bills and taxes on time, or do we ignore what is due?

A Couple Shares Their Experience: *"With our finances, we manage different parts of the responsibility, but each of us sees the money that goes in and out. We also made a pact that we would not purchase a major household item unless we both especially liked it, so we protected our unity. That meant it took a long time to replace our bedspread, but we both had to like it. If one person did not find a choice attractive, there was no pleading or bargaining, we just kept looking, showing, and consulting.*

"We looked for a year for bookshelves and still could not find the right thing. Then, one day, in the window of a furniture store, I saw a wonderful bookcase. It was perfect for the space and quite handsome. I called my partner and requested they go into this store and look. They came home later that day and said, 'Honey, did you really like that bookcase?'. I responded with 'Yes, I did!'. They happily said, 'Good, because I bought it!'. We are pleased to say that this happens to us often. If we are patient, we can find something we both like."

Effectively managing money relies greatly on the Character Quality of Dependability. It's an essential Quality when we have responsibilities, such as paying the family bills on time or managing the funds of a family member. In these cases, we have confidence in each other to carefully manage and account for money. We maintain our Trust in each other because we demonstrate financial Dependability.

Additional Character Qualities to take into consideration are Justice and Respect. Neither of us should feel like we are begging the other for money. It's also not a weapon to use against each other. Each of us is a full partner in making financial decisions and in setting guidelines for how we manage our money, regardless of how much or how little each of us earns. Both of us are full and equal partners with valuable roles, even if one of us makes more money than the other, and even if one of us is a stay-at-home parent and does not bring income into the relationship and family.

Future Planning

Another significant area of money management is our future. Many aspects of life will benefit from us saving and doing tax and estate planning, and not just spending.

Below are some examples:

- Vacations
- Buying a home
- Education
- Retirement
- Potential illness
- Caregiving help for ourselves or relatives

Managing money often requires sacrifice. We may sacrifice for our children to have the benefit of an experience, or we may sacrifice spending in the present to build for the future. Regular consultation balances the different needs of everyone in the family.

A Couple Shares Their Experience: *"Our marriage is a second one for both of us, so we came in with expectations of how we each liked to handle money. Early in the marriage, we held regular 'Economic Summits' where we consulted and figured out what we needed as a couple and what we needed as individuals. Over time, these consultations have led us to create a special account to save for vacations. As circumstances change, we adjust what we each contribute to our joint account. When we can accomplish our plans for our house and our family, it's very satisfying and brings us closer together as a couple."*

The degree of harmony that appears along with our couple consultations about money indicates whether money is a connecting item or a source of conflict for us:

> "The security and synergy of a committed financial partnership actually contributes to long-term financial success. Studies show that married people who behave as

true financial partners tend to do better financially. Sure, you can find exceptions, but overall, having a strong foundation in commitment increases the likelihood not only that you'll preserve your bond through the ups and downs on life's emotional roller-coaster but also that you'll be financially secure. So although you do take a risk when you tie your financial life to another in marriage, full financial partnership has its benefits."[76]
Natalie H. Jenkins, Scott M. Stanley, William C. Bailey, and Howard J. Markman

When we have big financial decisions to make or complex management issues to handle, we make wiser choices when we consult with an expert third party. At times we may also include others in consultations who would be affected by a decision of ours. Expanding our consultations with input from others results in good decisions that work for both or all of us. If we experience disunity, we can take a break and then resume later. We apply Perseverance over time until we arrive at solutions.

Examples:

- "We will pay our bills on time or make responsible arrangements for payments."
- "As each of our children is born, we will establish an education fund for them."
- "We will give ____% of our income to charities."
- "We will invest ____% of income for our future retirement."
- "We will save a portion of every amount we earn."

Applying Character Qualities:

Below are some practical ways to incorporate character into daily practices with the theme of this chapter.

Orderliness

- Organize files and records for efficient retrieval and for use by those who need access.
- Seek professional help with money management as needed.
- Carry out bookkeeping tasks, being responsible for managing the recordkeeping for accurate bill paying, banking, investing, taxes, and other financial transactions.

Self-Discipline

- Resist temptations to spend money outside of our agreed plan based on our shared values.
- Avoid arguments about money that harm our relationship and instead focus on consulting together to find agreement.
- Apply personal strengths and skills in striving for prosperity.

Trust

- Honestly share what we value most about money and how it's used.
- Avoid manipulating or subverting each other's true intentions with money.
- Communicate openly and regularly about personal financial history, income, debts, spending, passwords, and all money management topics. [***Caution:*** This should be paced with the stage of the relationship.]

Learning Activities:

1. Individually, write down our top three personal values that relate to money. Share and consult about them together. Next, determine the top three values related to money that we will hold as a couple going forward.

2. Consult and compile a list of the value statements that will contribute to our making harmonious decisions related to money.

   Examples of value statements:

   - "Our children's education is a vital investment."
   - "Being careful with spending will conserve our resources."
   - "If possible, we will financially support family members in need without requiring repayment."
   - "We will manage our finances with honesty and integrity."
   - "We will plan for our retirement."
   - "We will pay off all debts before we take a major vacation."
   - "We will contribute to charities as part of our community outreach."

3. Reflect and consult about the following topics over an agreed spread of time, where they apply to us:

   a. Who earns what and in what ways; How is money handled if there is only one income or one partner has an income that is higher than the other one has
   b. How much each can spend without consultation with each other first

c. How to pay the bills and who is responsible; How to save or invest funds; How to prepare for taxes
d. How much debt and risk are comfortable for each of us
e. Whether bank and investment accounts are separate, joint, or both
f. Whose name is shown as the owner on large items, such as vehicles and property
g. How or whether to budget; How much to donate to charities
h. How both are kept informed about the state of the finances
i. What is wasteful, generous, moderate, thrifty, or stingy
j. Who to loan money to or not loan to; who to borrow from or not borrow from
k. What insurance policies are necessary for us
l. What provisions are important to have in our wills and included in estate planning
m. What professionals are needed to support financial decisions and activities

4. Meet with a financial planner or certified financial educator/counselor to ensure we are organized about planning for our short- and long-term financial well-being and that of our family. If we are not able to afford a professional, then determine whether a family member or a friend could provide helpful input instead. Both may also be useful.

5. Annually check our credit and ability to borrow money, any retirement funds we may have or expect to have, our wills and estate plans, and the status of any long-term debts, such as a home mortgage or vehicle loan.

6. Assess whether our ability to earn or manage money is being affected by societal systems or institutions that are unjust or prejudiced and interfering with our ability to progress (Examples: access to loans, bank availability, hiring difficulties…). Make a plan that aligns with our Character Qualities and our values for how to address the issues we identify, involving others as needed.

Couple Reflection and Consultation:

Throughout this couple guide, there are invitations to practice the Character Quality of Reflection about your interactions and connection. This practice gives you opportunities to celebrate progress and consult to address issues.

1. What preparations and circumstances contribute to harmonious financial consultations between us?
2. What various emotions arise for us when we think about money?
3. What major experiences growing up and previously in our lives affect our financial attitudes and choices now? Is it wise to challenge or change any of our views and approaches that are based on the past?
4. What values related to money do we have in common? Which ones are different? How can we manage our different values?
5. What are our most important goals for saving money? How highly do we value saving and spending money for our children's education? To leave for relatives or charities when we die?
6. What motivates us with earning an income? What new efforts, if any, do we want to make in how we generate income?
7. What guidelines are useful for us about spending money?

8. What motivates us when giving money to charity? What guidelines do we use in choosing charities to donate to?
9. What are our attitudes about borrowing: from family members, from friends, by going into debt with credit cards, or through obtaining a loan from a financial institution?
10. What is the status of our credit—the ability to borrow money for large expenditures? Do we need to improve our credit? How can we do this?
11. What is our attitude about loaning money to others? Under what circumstances might we choose to do this?
12. When do we use a budget? How strictly do we follow it? How do we handle being over budget?
13. What financial management systems and tools do we have confidence in and use?
14. What family relationship do we want to acknowledge through bequests in our wills? By naming them as beneficiaries on financial accounts or insurance?
15. Who could dependably help us with financial decisions and management?

Vitalizer 16: Growing from Difficulties

"See difficulties as learning opportunities that will expand your talents and capacities. Remind yourself that you can positively influence much of what happens in life."
Stephen Post

Focus Statement: Throughout our life together, we will face many difficulties, and we commit to navigating them as partners through consultation and growing individually and together in the process.

Deeper Learning:

We can prevent some difficulties or moderate the impact of others when we study and learn new information ahead of time. We see this in action in our lives as we learn about staying unified and as we practice connection activities.

However, the nature of life is that it has difficulties—the small, the challenging, and the devastating. They can arise from outside of our relationship, and they also happen between us. We have greater strength when we face problems together.

Learning Opportunities

When we notice learning opportunities during and after difficulties, we see that we can:

- Strengthen a Character Quality to respond well
- Benefit from asking for help and working as a team
- Deepen our communications
- Build our resilience

It's vital to improve how we respond positively and maturely to make use of troubling situations. We can then foster our physical, mental, emotional, and spiritual growth as individuals and as a couple.

> "In exasperating situations, we must find the time to reflect if we are not afterwards to regret our words and actions. The Golden Rule, 'Do unto others what you would have them do unto you' or 'Do not do to others that which you do not wish done to yourself' is a useful guideline for action."[77] Mehri Sefidvash

When problems happen or we make a mistake, there is an opportunity to gain wisdom and practice good judgment. While "he" is used in this quotation, the information applies to a partner as well:

> "When faced with a problem, the spiritually immature person tries to escape. Instead of facing the problem, he hopes that someone else will resolve it, or that it will just go away. If he has committed an error, he blames another. If someone else commits an error, he attaches great importance to it and has a hard time forgiving. Instead of trying to find a solution to the problem, he concentrates on its cause, blaming persons or circumstances other than himself.
>
> "In contrast, the spiritually mature person faces whatever problems arise with relative calm and decision. He recognizes and acknowledges whatever faults he may have committed which have contributed to the problem and accepts and forgives the errors made by others. He doesn't get bogged down in talking about who caused the problem or waste energy defending himself. He concentrates on searching for a good solution, using prayer

for divine guidance, meditation, and consultation with others. Then he willingly cooperates in carrying out the actions necessary to apply the solution."[78]
Joan B. Hernández

Unified Response to Difficulties

Every problem has unique aspects to it, and most will require specialized approaches. However, whatever the difficulty, we must apply our Unity to address it together as companions. Facing problems together as a couple helps us:

- Share our thoughts
- Heal our wounds
- Address our fears
- Renew our love
- Strengthen our Trust

We improve our response to difficulties, as well as our vitality and connection, when we use the Character Quality of Reflection and the communication skill of consultation. We use these approaches to give each other time to think and understand what is happening. Together we come up with practical solutions neither of us would have created on our own. [See "Core Element B: Reflection and Consultation".]

Some problems are more like regular irritants that we must determine how to handle. For example, we know that fluctuating hormone levels can cause mood swings and physical symptoms, such as pain or the inability to function as well as we want. Variations like this in our well-being are continually an opportunity to practice Qualities like Flexibility and Compassion.

A Couple Shares Their Experience: *"Every month as my partner's hormones kicked in before her menstrual period, I became tense. She often became critical of things that normally she easily ignored. She got angry and tearful. We both were very stressed about these experiences. It took some time and effort, but we searched for all types of solutions for how to make this time of the month easier for us both, and we implemented some changes. It helped that we looked at this as something for us to address as a couple and not just a problem for her to handle."*

However, many problems are more major, and many of them can have aspects of loss and grief. Here are helpful ways to respond:

> "Keep the channels of communication clear. Without an open and honest dialogue, a husband and wife will unknowingly build barriers around their hearts. They will journey separate paths and lose touch with one another. … Keeping communication channels open requires vulnerability. It demands your real feelings. It assumes your tears will roll down each other's cheeks."[79]
> Les and Leslie Parrott

A Couple Shares Their Experience: *"We struggled in the early years of our marriage with not being able to have a child. Dealing with infertility left us with sadness, frustration, and misunderstandings. Our relationship became more about trying to have a child than anything else. We recognized we needed professional help, and that we needed to be back focused on our friendship and connection. Being re-connected helped us consult about new solutions. Today we have two healthy children, and we are stronger together as a couple."*

Recovery Afterward

Recovery takes different lengths of time, depending on the severity of the challenge and the maturity of our skills. Everyday issues do not take much time for us to work through them. However, for more serious difficulties:

> "Good marriages that have bumped into bad things do not recover quickly. Not generally, anyway. And smart couples do not buy into instant success plans that promise hurried ways to heal hearts or rapid roads to renewed relationships. They know better and, instead, expect slow progress, steadily building one marriage accomplishment upon another, like a game that is won one play at a time, or a building that is built brick by brick."[80]
> Les and Leslie Parrott

When we know we have had a difficulty that will take time to recover from, we do our best to apply Compassion and Flexibility with each other. We may not be thinking as clearly as usual from stress, so we try out healing solutions and review how they are working. We can then adjust and try new approaches and behaviors.

A Couple Shares Their Experience: *"One of the thorniest problems for us to consult through has been infidelity, and our issues were charged and intense. A professional therapist assisted us as well; we could not have succeeded without that. During and after therapy, we had to face each other and figure out a way to utilize consultation to maintain unity in our marriage. We needed a big space for consulting, and so we did most of it on walks outside. This gave each of us the chance to say what we needed to say. We had the space and distance to* *process our feelings and consider our options and responses without having to immediately speak.*

"As we walked, we were mindful of each other's emotional needs and state. Each of us had permission to say that we needed time to process our feelings and were not in a space to listen. Each of us had permission to say that we would not speak unless we knew that the other person was present in the moment. We wanted each other to be receptive to utilizing whatever comments came forth to keep our marriage together. When we began sharing or listening, if our feelings changed, we let the other person know.

"Once we decided to try to work through the infidelity and rebuild our marriage, each of us acted fully toward that end. We demonstrated Respect for each person's needs, including giving them time to process and understand what the other said. Sometimes this required time alone or bringing up the same point in a slightly different way several times to gain understanding. Sometimes it meant releasing resentment, fear, and sorrow, and we gave the space to be sad. We needed time and space for each of us to process our feelings, to grieve, and to forgive. While consultation is used to 'solve' something, it's also a vehicle to get to truth. We use it to discover our own personal truths by sharing our thoughts and feelings and remaining open to one another's insights."

Life Is a Learning Experience

As we experience difficulties and work through them together, we realize that life is a learning-in-action process. This realization makes it easier to relax and not try so hard to be perfect. We can bravely step forward to try something new with less worry about failure or criticism from each other or others. It's also easier to accept a mistake if we learn from it.

If we focus as individuals on growing our Character Qualities in response to challenges, we will achieve victories and growth. As we go through difficulties, our self-confidence grows, and we gain a mental toughness that can push us through the next one that comes. We learn what we can do, and this spreads to all areas of our life.

We strive to have the following be our attitude:

> "See difficulties as learning opportunities that will expand your talents and capacities. Remind yourself that you can positively influence much of what happens in life. See yourself as capable and as an active participant in your world. Even when a problem has aspects that cannot be changed, trust that if you are resourceful, you will be able to use the situation to learn new ways of responding to it. Welcome change and challenge. Have faith that greater life meaning and satisfaction will emerge from each stressful situation."[81] Stephen Post

Even when we know the best ways to behave to maintain our relationship, we are still likely to struggle to carry them out at times. Our goal as human beings is always to demonstrate Excellence, but perfection is not possible. Failures, which happen to everyone, strengthen our Humility and Trust in our ability to resolve the issues and rebound. [See "Vitalizer 17: Resolving and Rebounding".]

Difficulties provide opportunities to ask for help, make amends, and learn new ways of speaking and acting. Problems give us opportunities to strengthen our characters and make better choices the next time. Addressing issues rather than hiding from them increases the possibility of having a stronger, happier couple relationship.

Examples:

- "I am angry and devastated that my job has ended."
- "Moving to be near our families is raising many issues from my childhood."
- "Our bank balance is getting very low, what will we do?"
- "The doctor says the lump is cancerous."
- "I have become dependent on drinking alcohol every day after work."
- "The car has a flat tire, and the spare tire is missing."

Applying Character Qualities:

Below are some practical ways to incorporate character into daily practices with the theme of this chapter.

Compassion

- Listen carefully to each other's sharing about experiences and responses to difficulties.
- Offer comforting and supportive words.
- Reach out to offer assistance, waiting to hear from the other what is truly helpful.

Flexibility

- Adjust to a "new normal" when change happens.
- Make new plans when the first ones cannot happen.
- Hold ourselves still and quiet instead of rushing into a response.

Humility

- Acknowledge some happenings in life are difficult and not our preference.

- Carry out tasks that we are not used to doing when our help is needed.
- Accept our limitations and that we sometimes each have different approaches to tasks and problems.

Learning Activities:

1. Identify a problem from the past and assess the learning or skill-building that came from it. Identify a current problem that could benefit from the learning and apply it.

2. Assess how hormones affect our functioning. Choose two actions to address or improve our health or reactions to how hormones affect us.

3. Plan and carry out a trip, looking ahead for what difficulties might arise and preparing for them. When difficulties arise, consult and work together to face them. After the trip, reflect on whether we were able to apply Flexibility and Unity. What did we learn from the experience?

4. Choose a home project to cooperate on accomplishing together. Set a target completion date and agreed-on action steps to get there. Carry the project out. Reflect and consult with each other throughout to determine the next steps. What went well? What were the difficulties? How did we handle them?

5. Evaluate a current difficult situation. What Character Qualities could we apply to improve it? What learning is happening?

Couple Reflection and Consultation:

Throughout this couple guide, there are invitations to practice the Character Quality of Reflection about your interactions and connection. This practice gives you opportunities to celebrate progress and consult to address issues.

1. How do we generally respond to difficulties that arise?
2. If we spend time together dealing with a problem or emergency, does this bring us closer together? Why or why not? What supports us in staying connected and respond as a united couple to a difficulty?
3. What have we learned from a difficulty in the past? When have we successfully used learning from a difficult situation in new circumstances?
4. When has denial or temporary avoidance allowed us to gather our inner resources to cope with a difficulty? When does avoidance become unhealthy, such as turning to alcohol, drugs, shopping, sex, or other means of trying to ignore what happened or is currently happening?
5. What do we want to improve about our responses to difficulties?
6. What are some character strengths we have used well in difficulties?
7. What specific Character Qualities have we strengthened from working through a difficulty?
8. What Character Qualities have we discovered are weaker as we respond to difficulties? How will we strengthen them to be more effective during the next difficulty?
9. When have we found it useful to turn to professionals to help us manage a difficulty? What was the outcome?
10. When have we successfully reached out and found help from others, such as family or friends, or accepted offered help when a problem was happening?

Vitalizer 17: Resolving and Rebounding

"Being kind and generous as well as granting pardon will put you back on the same footing and keep your love strong."
H. J. Markman, S. M. Stanley, S. L. Blumberg, N. H. Jenkins, and C. Whiteley

Focus Statement: We actively resolve issues, forgive with our minds and hearts, resiliently bounce back, and maintain our unity.

Deeper Learning:

When we truly address, repair, and resolve issues, they do not keep coming back to disrupt our relationship. When we choose to forgive and let go of hurt feelings, we create a space for unity to reappear and disunity to dissipate. It's wise to keep our life as "cleaned up" as possible, no matter what the size of the issue.

Resolving issues includes being effective at:

- Reflecting and consulting to understand what happened and why, including identifying whether there was a vital need not being met
- Applying our Humility and acknowledging our errors; noting where our words or actions caused hurt feelings or problems
- Regretting what happened; repenting
- Cleaning up whatever problems we have caused or are partially responsible for
- Asking each other for forgiveness
- Truly granting pardon so that our minds and hearts are calm, and we put the issue in the past

- Learning from what occurred and from the clean-up process
- Applying the learning to demonstrate improved behaviors
- Demonstrating Respect for ourselves and acknowledging our efforts to grow
- Being resilient in continuing with our relationship in a healthy way

The longer we stay stuck in whatever poor choice we made and its consequences, the deeper the hole we dig. We become emotionally and mentally stuck in the past, and this influences our present, future, and often our involvement in many aspects of life. Progress takes courage. Making efforts to resolve what happened and resiliently go forward empowers us to have a better present and future. We are lighter and happier when not dragging unresolved issues along with us.

Forgiveness

Forgiveness is a crucial component in resolving issues, although it's often very difficult to do. Counselor and marriage educator Michele Weiner-Davis is very direct with couples about why it's so important:

> "Don't pretend that you are putting effort into your marriage when you have a mental ledger book detailing your spouse's every wrongdoing. As long as you are holding on to resentments of the past, you can't be forgiving. As long as you are not forgiving, you can't be loving. As long as you aren't loving, you can't do what it takes to make your marriage work. So decide. Are you going to carry a grudge and stand by while you and your spouse become a divorce statistic or are you going to rid yourself of the shackles of the past which have held you

prisoner? Forgive your spouse and start anew."[82] Michele Weiner-Davis

We can describe forgiveness in many ways. Some of these are:

- Pardoning someone for saying or doing something hurtful or harmful
- Giving up a desire for revenge
- Letting go of anger and resentment

Bravely requesting and offering forgiveness to each other strengthens our Respect and Unity. We notice that our missteps become learning, which then feeds into actions that benefit us and others. It can be powerful for us to look back at something that has transformed since we failed or caused harm. [See "Vitalizer 16: Growing from Difficulties".]

If our words or actions harmed each other or others, we may feel that we cannot ask for forgiveness, or the issue may not feel complete until we clean up the problems we caused. There are usually concrete actions we can take to resolve issues that arose from our behavior. We need to ensure, however, that any remedial actions we consider will not cause further harm. This includes not causing harm to ourselves. We demonstrate Respect and maintain our dignity in the process of addressing the situation.

We may find these five ways of carrying out a forgiveness process useful, as suggested by the authors of *When Sorry Isn't Enough*:

1. Expressing Regret: "I am sorry."
2. Accepting Responsibility: "I was wrong."
3. Making Restitution: "What can I do to make it right?"
4. Genuinely Repenting: "I want to change."

5. Requesting Forgiveness: "Can you find it in your heart to forgive me?"

The authors suggest that many factors are important to consider when offering an apology. These are summarized below.

- Our tone of voice and body language must match our words for the receiver to believe that our apology is sincere.
- State specifically what the apology is for and acknowledge the hurt caused.
- Avoid any language such as "...but..." that communicates blame to the person to whom we are apologizing; attacks or defensiveness do not usually lead to forgiveness and reconciliation.
- Do not use apology to try to manipulate someone; for example, apologizing in the hope that the recipient will change some behavior.
- Depending on the circumstances and relationship, we may find it most effective to put our apology in writing.[83]

Summarized from Gary Chapman and Jennifer Thomas

Forgiveness is not the same as ignoring the situation or saying that what happened was okay. The initial problem still needs to be addressed—just as we are responsible for our own actions, so are others for theirs. The next step then, of course, is for us to be clear about what behaviors to improve and begin to address them. This fuels our resiliency and recovery.

A Couple Shares Their Experience: *"We both love to be helpful to each other. However, we have learned that it's wise and demonstrates Respect to consult with each other before* *jumping in with unasked-for assistance. One incident made this understanding clear to us.*

"We were both working in the yard in different places. I went up the ladder with an electric trimmer and began cutting off branches of a tree. I let them fall to the ground. My partner saw what I was doing, came over, and began gathering up the fallen branches and moving around the base of the ladder.

"Unfortunately, they bumped a shoulder up against the ladder, which distracted me and made me feel unsafe. As I moved in response, I cut the electrical cord attached to the trimmer. This tripped the power off to our whole home, and I came close to falling from the ladder. I yelled, 'You could have waited to clean up until after I was done!'. I was angry and upset.

"Later that day, after we calmed down and we were able to talk about the situation, my partner said, 'I'm sorry for getting in the way and causing the accident.' I responded with, 'I forgive you. And…I'm sorry I yelled at you.'

"We consulted about what had happened and how to prevent a repeat incident. We realized we had skipped consulting with each other about responsibilities before going outside to work. I was also able to share that it would have worked better for me if we had consulted briefly about the timing of the help before it started."

Forgiveness frees us from holding against someone what they did. Forgiving is choosing to reject "vengeance, renounce bitterness, break the silence of estrangement, and actually wish the best" for the other person.[84] (Les and Leslie Parrott) It takes courage for us to ask for forgiveness and apply our Compassion to grant it, especially when what seemed to have happened felt unfair. It takes courage to address the issues so that it feels like fairness and unity have been re-established. It takes both our minds and our hearts to accomplish the task.

Courage and love are interlinked:

> "Courage is love as action—love on her silver steed, forcing change in the world, rising to challenges, negotiating life with skill, and confronting others with care and wisdom. The qualities that courage draws upon—hardiness and resilience, as well as the ability to bend and alter course when faced with difficulty, to commit oneself to a cause, and to find inner power during times of pain—are *all* associated with mental health. We need a deep, tensile strength to face the tough times in life, to speak out persuasively against injustice, and, above all, to love others wisely and well. To love at all is a risk that requires courage—we risk our safety, letting ourselves be raw and vulnerable; we accept our share of compromise and weather disappointment and despair; and above all, we are willing to confront a loved one even if what we need to say is not easy or kind."[85] Stephen Post

This perspective addresses applying both our minds and our hearts:

> "When you forgive, you need to do more than say the words and mean them. You also have to extend a forgiving, helping hand. To truly forgive, you need to be gracious to your partner. Being kind and generous as well as granting pardon will put you back on the same footing and keep your love strong."[86] Howard J. Markman, Scott M. Stanley, Susan L. Blumberg, Natalie H. Jenkins, and Carol Whiteley

Forgiveness needs to be sincere and honest. It's not wise to forgive someone automatically just because the situation is difficult, or because we feel unhappy that the other person is regretful. If we say we forgive someone while we are still holding onto considerable anger, sadness, or pain from the incident, the situation will not be easily resolved. Some inner healing likely needs to happen first.

Once a situation is resolved, then we need to leave it in the past and not bring it up again. Reminding someone about the situation can indicate that we did not completely forgive the first time, and we interfere with rebounding and re-building. Of course, we are also engaged in the necessary behavior adjustments and making amends, so similar situations drop in frequency and then stop occurring.

Caution: When there are serious issues between you, such as infidelity, or there are repeated and serious misbehaviors, mental illnesses, or crimes, please seek professional assistance and/or help from civil authorities.

Bouncing Back Afterward

Here is a perspective about resilient people. They:

> "... have three distinguishing characteristics: an acceptance of reality, a strongly held belief that life is meaningful, and an ability to find creative solutions to seemingly insoluble problems."[87] Janet A. Khan

People practice resilience effectively when they:

- Accept and adjust to change rather than resisting it
- Act calmly during crises and take positive steps to manage them
- Seek creative and appropriate solutions to problems
- Learn from challenges to prevent them from reoccurring or to improve responses in the future
- Adapt to changing circumstances

- Remain calm so that their thinking stays clear, and they respond effectively
- Stay engaged, optimistic, and aware when faced with difficult events or experiences
- Process, grieve, and recover from failures, disruptive events, losses, and disappointments; confidently re-focus on goals and resume action

A Reflection

When we value our unity and decrease our tolerance for disunity, we are motivated to seek resolution. We address issues as needed so they do not linger and harm our relationship. Our commitment to unity assists us to be thorough with our forgiveness process. Our focused attention on healing positions us to resiliently bounce back.

Examples:

- "I know my anger at my mother's behavior keeps coming out as attacks on you—I agree to go to counseling sessions to address this—please forgive me for hurting you."
- "I was not paying enough attention when I was cleaning the garage, and I threw away something important to you—I am very sorry I did that. Please forgive me. I know it will not be the same, but may I buy a new one for you?"
- "I forgot to pick up your medicine from the store when I drove past—I apologize, and I will go back right away."
- "Our current way of handling the bills is not working for me, because we keep getting behind on them, and I get angry every time. Can we please consult about a new approach?"

Applying Character Qualities:

Below are some practical ways to incorporate character into daily practices with the theme of this chapter.

Compassion

- See beyond the immediate actions the other took and look at the whole person and the context of their lives, holding a spirit of goodwill that the other did not intend to cause the harm that happened.
- Acknowledge the inner pain each feels and behave gently and kindly to begin healing.
- Release attachment to what happened and consciously be open to lovingly re-connect.

Perseverance

- Recognize when forgiveness is a process that will take time, and we stay engaged for as long as is needed with carrying out all possible actions to clean up the situation and bring it to completion.
- Keep making efforts to improve communications and behaviors.
- Identify and carry out actions to resiliently rebound.

Unity

- See the bigger picture of the whole relationship and value it rather than holding onto resentment or grudges and building walls between us.
- Consciously observe the thoughts and emotions that are in the way of reuniting, acknowledge them, and do our best to let them go.
- Address any areas where we need to apply Justice, consulting together to determine new behaviors that are fair to both of us and will lead to resiliency and harmony.

Learning Activities:

1. Identify an issue that is still somewhat unresolved, identify remediating actions to take that will not likely cause harm, and take concrete steps toward forgiveness and healing. Consult and reflect on the situation and outcome, capture any learning, and determine what will prevent something like this from occurring again.

2. Create a healing ceremony for moving forward after an issue. Examples of elements that could be included are music, prayer, dancing or other movements, writing down issues or concerns and burning them, using water to cleanse our hands or bodies, and so on.

3. Identify an incident from the past and the learning that came from it. Consult and agree on how that learning can contribute to others or is actively contributing. Take at least one action step to benefit another person or pause to celebrate the contributions already underway.

4. Identify an issue that has been forgiven but we are not as re-connected as we want to be. Take two concrete action steps to feel closer together.

Couple Reflection and Consultation:

Throughout this couple guide, there are invitations to practice the Character Quality of Reflection about your interactions and connection. This practice gives you opportunities to celebrate progress and consult to address issues.

1. What supports us to effectively cope during times of stress caused when one of us unintentionally does something hurtful to the other?
2. Why is it important that forgiveness comes from both our minds and our hearts?
3. When we are tempted to raise a previously settled issue, what can stop us? When might it be important to refer to a previous issue, instead?
4. How can being committed to unity between us facilitate us offering forgiveness and agreeing to forgive?
5. If it feels like there is pressure to forgive before we are ready, how does this affect us and the situation? What Character Qualities can help us wait?
6. When can we use humor at times, so we handle difficult situations more lightly?
7. How could practicing gratitude for our blessings contribute to our well-being while resolving issues?
8. How could sincerely practicing Service for each other help us throughout the forgiveness and rebounding process?
9. What are practical ways we can reconnect after something harmful has happened?
10. What approaches increase our resilience after we have resolved an issue?

Section 6:

Expanding Beyond Us

Section 6 Introduction

As a couple, you interact with an expanded circle of many other people. Some you see only occasionally, but others you are with daily. The strength of your union and your couple vitality assist you to have constructive relationships with others.

From the foundation of unity, commitment, and cooperation you are building, you become a rich resource and example to your family, friends, and community. Your children thrive on the security of knowing you are deeply connected and love one another. You build friendships that enrich your lives, and you maintain a home that you are happy inviting others into. You offer the gifts of your Compassion and caring to those in your community. You have the well-being and strength to contribute to the lives of others.

Here in Section 6, you will expand your couple circle to include others:

- Vitalizer 18: Establishing Family Unity
- Vitalizer 19: Connecting with Friends and Community

Vitalizer 18: Establishing Family Unity

"At the center of...expanding concentric circles of unity is the family, and the foundation of the family is the relationship between the wife and husband."
Raymond and Furugh Switzer

Focus Statement: We value building unity in our family relationships, demonstrating Respect to those connected to us, spending time with them, and treating them well.

Deeper Learning:

As a couple, we are in a primary relationship, and our unity and connection are foundational and vital. Adding children expands our circle of unity, and we refer to ourselves as a family. The more complex our family becomes, the greater the challenges we sometimes experience in maintaining unity, and this will be explored later in this chapter. [More about family unity is also in "Core Element A: Commitment to Unity".]

Being Unified Parents

How we function as a family with children who live with us is an important focus for us to remember to keep positive, healthy, and well-functioning. We consult about how to parent well, and we learn from experienced people how to effectively provide discipline, education, and positive activities. We also reach out for help as needed.

A Couple Shares Their Experience: *"In the weeks after our daughter was born, we felt like we were moving in a fog of exhaustion. Other than an occasional hug, we barely felt like a couple. Then one morning after a few hours of sleep, we* *realized we missed each other! We consulted with my mother, who lived nearby. She agreed to come over after the baby was asleep and be there for an hour. We only went to a local restaurant for dessert, but that was enough to remind us that we had non-baby things to talk about and a friendship and couple relationship to maintain.*

"We committed to go out on dates every few weeks, and we have kept it up through the arrival of a second child and several years of parenting. It was one of the best decisions we ever made. Our children are happier when they see us happy together. They know we are united, and so they do not try to get one of us to make a decision without agreement from the other. We see them thriving in school and with friendships, in part because they do not feel anxiety about their home situation."

Parenting is not easy, but we view it as a vitally important responsibility. As our children grow, we guide them with making positive choices. We see discipline as teaching, not punishment:

> "The goal of effective parental authority is to enable children to develop their own inner authority, a sense of personal responsibility, and an ability to make conscious moral choices. The younger children are, the more dependent they are on a fair and loving parent to guide and discipline their behavior. Clear, reasonable discipline gives children the foundation for self-discipline. ... The patterns of behavior an educative parent focuses on are the virtues [character]."[88] Linda Kavelin Popov

As our children grow, we consult with them about simple choices. As they mature, perhaps by about age 5, we introduce them to family consultation. We hold family meetings as needed to ensure everyone has a voice in consulting about matters that affect some or all of us. This gives all of us the opportunity to practice leading a meeting, speaking, listening, taking notes, making decisions, and planning.

> "What the children appreciate about family meetings: Provides a safe space to express their feelings, gives them a chance to have their voice heard and their ideas discussed, creates a sense of belonging and purpose, provides experiences of making progress together, and involves everyone in planning for family activities."[89] Monette Van Lith

If one of us is troubled, we practice Compassion and offer support. We are loyal to each other and protect each other from harm. We do our best to spend enjoyable time as a family in many activities.

Our Extended Family

When we have positive relationships with our extended family members, it's easier for us to reach out for support from them:

> "In these vital and nurturing families, I consistently see a different pattern:
>
> - Self-worth is high.
> - Communication is direct, clear, specific, and honest.
> - Rules are flexible, human, appropriate, and subject to change.
> - The link to society is open and hopeful and is based on choice.

> "The changes all rest on new learnings, new awareness and a new consciousness. Everyone can achieve these."[90]
> Virginia Satir

Our extended family includes our parents, grandparents, aunts, uncles, and cousins. We may have stepparents and step- or half-siblings, which expands our family further. In-laws are another element to consider. All of these individuals may have family members who connect with us. How we build family unity with everyone can be energizing and wonderful. It can also feel challenging at times.

Our experiences growing up and the current quality of our family relationships affect the health and unity of our couple relationship. Many family members are troubled rather than unified, and we may find it difficult to live with or be around each other at times. Perhaps some of our family members behave in public like everything is fine but in private they behave very differently, and we feel like we have aspects of family life that are secret. We may experience some degree of absentee, neglectful, mentally ill, arguing, abusive, or violent family members. We reach out to mental health professionals to assist us when we are in very difficult circumstances.

Where an unhealthy family has been our experience while growing up, we will likely find it more difficult to find our way as a couple at times. We have more learning and growing to do to be successful.

If our family situation is or has been difficult, we may notice how it affects our moods and behavior. When extended family members get angry or criticize, we can use our Creativity to find constructive ways to reduce our anger and stress levels. We can comfort and support each other, but it's wise to avoid criticizing the family member. Sometimes in very difficult or abusive circumstances, it's only possible to contribute to family unity when there is no contact, and we simply send positive thoughts or say prayers for each other. We may also need professional assistance to guide us in learning how to respond constructively in these situations.

One aspect of interacting with family members is that when we are so close, it becomes easy to see each other's faults and failings. Focusing on these can become more dominant than seeing each other's good actions. Shifting to appreciate the positive in each person can improve our attitude toward them. [See "Vitalizer 8: Appreciating One Another".]

Who Is Family?

We may ask ourselves at times, "Who counts as my family?" For example, in stepfamilies, according to Maggie Scarf, author of *Remarriage Blueprint*, the "insider/outsider" forces are powerful. They often challenge the ideal of family unity and the ability of subsequent relationships or marriages to be healthy and stay intact. People hold loyalties to previous family members, and new members added in can cause polarized positions.

Families have cultures and mixing these up into new arrangements can at times cause emotional disruptions, pain, and disunity. How a couple disciplines children, the way money is shared among family members, time with former family members, the way celebrations are handled, and more can be quite complicated in blended families. There are extensive resources available for these types of family situations, so we access them as needed.

As we strive to build unity with blended family members, we can consider such behaviors as:

- Having a positive attitude
- Greeting one another pleasantly

- Demonstrating Respect for each other's living area and possessions
- Accepting each other's preferences
- Having meals with each other
- Reaching out consistently with positive communications
- Praying together
- Sharing activities
- Preserving original family memorabilia
- Telling stories about positive family experiences
- Helping each other with tasks
- Acknowledging and celebrating positive progress

Many of these techniques can also be valuable in non-blended families.

A Larger Circle of Unity

We have begun to see that the unity in our couple relationship and family provides part of the foundation for the broader unity of our community and the family of humanity. This topic is addressed in the next chapter, "Vitalizer 19: Connecting with Friends and Community".

As we look for opportunities to interact in harmony within our family—whatever its strengths, construction, or issues—we can learn what it takes to stay united. This will contribute to our ability to build unity with others. Here is a broader view of the importance of marriage and family:

> "Humanity has developed through different stages of groupings: families, clans, tribes, villages, cities, nation states, and, now, the whole world. At the center of these expanding concentric circles of unity is the family, and the foundation of the family is the relationship between the wife and husband. Our understanding is that marriage

holds within it the seed of the wider unity and is a significant working ground for this ultimate goal. From this perspective we can see how marriage functions not only for the best interests of both partners and their offspring, but that it also serves a higher, more expansive purpose....”[91] Raymond and Furugh Switzer

It's our goal to be a happy and unified family that is involved in education, work, and community service. Harmony, unity, well-being, and love are high ideals in human relationships, especially in a family, and it takes our focused effort to create them. Positive relationships within our home can also extend outward to include others we consider as family. Our ability to reach out and include others in our lives enriches us, and we all develop family relationship skills.

A Couple Shares Their Experience: *“There are many everyday occurrences that often result in happiness, smiles, or laughter for me: hugging and cuddling with my partner, watching our children get along and help around the house, watching humorous videos, cuddling with our cat, reading, telling jokes, cooking yummy food, listening to fun music together, tickling my kids, and visiting or chatting with friends and family.”*

Examples:

- Teach children a new skill.
- Have a regular meal with our extended family members.
- Share tasks related to caring for our older family members.
- Help each other with major home maintenance tasks.
- Hold regular family meetings.

Applying Character Qualities:

Below are some practical ways to incorporate character into daily practices with the theme of this chapter.

Dependability

- Make and keep promises and commitments that build our ability to rely on each other.
- Handle responsibilities for keeping our family going in a positive direction.
- Set and maintain consistent standards for learning and behaviors for our children.

Flexibility

- Accept and adjust to each other's personality, using gentle humor as needed.
- Arrange times for family members to be together, even when it's difficult to coordinate.
- Adjust to major life events such as illness, death, moving, or new family members, striving to maintain connection and love throughout, and being open to occasional positive surprises.

Service

- Consult with appropriate family members about what actions they consider helpful and their preferences for what happens in our family and home.
- Carry out thoughtful actions for family members that align with their needs and wishes, learning to do new actions as needed.
- Express gratitude consistently for the words and actions each of us carries out to benefit our family members and extended family relationships.

Learning Activities:

1. Create a family mission statement, with our children as appropriate. "A family mission statement is a combined, unified expression from all family members of what your family is all about—what it is you really want to do and be—and the principles you choose to govern your family life."[92] Stephen R. Covey

2. Write a list of what we appreciate about each of our children, parents, grandparents, siblings, and other close family members, focusing on those that are alive. If applicable, also write a list of what we appreciate, or appreciated in the past, about the relationship between us and our close family members.

3. Create a video of our family or a collection of photos that represents a mix of the high and low points of our family life. Share it with someone close to us and use the experience to reflect in a balanced way on our experiences. If appropriate and positive, we will share what we created with family members.

4. Collect a few positive or quirky family stories that demonstrate our family's culture. Create a family gathering and share the stories or share them at an occasion we attend.

5. Create a meal and serve it to our extended family members.

6. Establish a pattern of holding family meetings, involving all those living in our home according to their capacities.

7. Work with our children to create drawings or greeting cards for older family members and deliver or mail them.

8. Plan a celebration that includes elements of the ethnic culture of one or more family members.

Couple Reflection and Consultation:

Throughout this couple guide, there are invitations to practice the Character Quality of Reflection about your interactions and connection. This practice gives you opportunities to celebrate progress and consult to address issues.

1. How do we describe our family?
2. What do we like about our relationship with our children?
3. What is working well in educating and encouraging our children to have many character strengths? What do we want to improve? How will we accomplish that?
4. What does family unity mean to us? How can we foster greater family unity?
5. What do we appreciate about our relationships with other family members?
6. What is difficult in our family relationships? How can we address or overcome the difficulties? What do we simply need to accept?
7. What Character Qualities do we choose as our guides for our immediate family? For our extended family?
8. What boundaries are wise for us to have in place to prevent harm to us from problematic family members?
9. What thoughtful actions can we offer to various family members? How will we carry them out?
10. What gets in the way of our demonstrating Respect and courtesy to family members? How could we practice Unity in more of our interactions?

Vitalizer 19: Connecting with Friends and Community

"Offering whatever we can in the spirit of sharing and service, and also of joint experience, is also part of hospitality."
Agnes Ghaznavi

Focus Statement: We are a strong and unified couple with vital connections with our friends, neighbors, and the community around us, and we actively spend time with them for our mutual well-being.

Deeper Learning:

When we have positive relationships with our friends and neighbors it contributes to us being healthy and happy as a couple. Sometimes building those relationships feels easy to do and it's energizing. However, exhaustion or focus on our responsibilities and activities can make it feel difficult to participate. We stay in action though, as we do see there is a necessary balance between managing our own lives and being part of the lives of others. This balance contributes to achieving couple vitality and well-being.

As we consult about what is important to us and how to use our available time, we use Creativity to find ways to foster our connection with others. We have mutual and separate friends who are supporters of our union, and we schedule time with them. We know who many of our neighbors are, and we do our best to apply Friendliness and interact with them well. As we reach out to neighbors and friends, it draws us together. We also gain people to celebrate with and help us during difficulties. This network of people is also positioned to collaborate in building a better community around us.

Expanding Friendships

When we reflect on our life, we realize that sometimes our circle of people is too limited. It can take courage to build new friend or neighbor relationships that enrich our lives. We can experience barriers at times, such as prejudices, lack of financial resources, competition, comparison, fear of rejection, shortage of time and energy, discomfort about our home and environment, and more. How can we overcome barriers like these? What is important to us? What personal growth and couple strengthening would assist us to connect with new people?

Involvement with friends and other people in a community can enrich communications we have as a couple, keep us growing as individuals, and connect us when we participate together. We could join a book discussion, exercise club, community theater, sports team, game-playing gatherings, or any other group that interests us. (*Possible resource to use:* https://www.meetup.com/.)

We notice that it's also good for us to form friendships with other couples that we both like and enjoy. It can be difficult to find these but well worth the time investment, as we can have fun together and support each other in having healthy relationships. We can validate that some challenges we have are normal, and we can problem-solve together, while still maintaining appropriate privacy.

Hospitality

We began to consult about hospitality in "Vitalizer 11: Enjoying Social Time". When our relationship and family life feel harmonious and connected, it can be an extension of our happiness to invite others into our home. We can relax and get to know others, share with them what is important to us, and enjoy building friendships.

> "Sharing is part of hospitality, not only materially but also spiritually: the atmosphere, the qualities of the members of the household. Learning is another aspect: 'peeping in at the window' into another family's way of living is the privilege and benefit of the guests. Offering whatever we can in the spirit of sharing and service, and also of joint experience, is also part of hospitality. Hospitality in the home is a most important way of learning about the outside world. People bring into the home other customs, opinions and ways of doing things, and children as well as adults widen their horizons in increased understanding of the world of human beings."[93] Agnes Ghaznavi

As we connect while offering hospitality, conversations may naturally flow into consulting about how to contribute to each other, our shared neighborhood, or the wider community.

The Wider Community

Community building and betterment are ways that our unity as a couple can contribute to others. These might include our reaching out to neighbors, other parents, colleagues, and more to establish cooperative working relationships or true friendships. We learn that we can collaborate with a very diverse set of people and become friends in the process. Our interactions can include meaningful conversations, fun social time and laughter, creative activities that benefit our neighborhood or community, education support for children and youth, and more.

Community building that includes laughter could look like this:

> "Like a good roll of duct tape, humor bonds us to each other. It strengthens us as a community, and it allows us to transcend our differences and our barriers. … Only when we can get past ourselves, when we can laugh past our perceived superiority and righteousness, can we truly look at our neighbor with a sense of hospitality and justice. … We all laugh in the same language…. When we laugh together, we not only cross barriers, but we also bond together as community."[94] Susan Sparks

We know that practicing Service toward each other is a vital and healthy element of our relationship. [See "Vitalizer 13: Giving Thoughtful Service".] Looking outward then includes us choosing to demonstrate Service to others. Acting to better the community around us trains us to consult in groups, collaborate to accomplish tasks, and think selflessly about the needs of others—a great skill in a family.

Engaging in practicing Service means that we move beyond our self-centered activities and concerns. When we serve people together, it can lift our minds, hearts, and souls to a higher level, and it can strengthen our couple relationship. However, we must remember to use Moderation so we continue to meet the needs of our relationship, family, and home.

A Couple Shares Their Experience: *"When we began our relationship, we identified that it was important for us to do activities that contributed to others and to observe how we collaborated. After some investigation of ideas, we determined that we were living in an area that had frequent severe storms but an inadequate emergency plan in place. We observed that* *one of us is comfortable in a leadership position, and the other prefers to work behind the scenes, and we valued both. It was extraordinarily satisfying to us both to create a coalition of people from the government and community and develop a response plan together.*

"Now that we are in a committed relationship, community service is integrated into who we are and what we do. It's a passion that energizes us and draws us together in unity."

When we practice Humility and Respect during community service, we:

- Build friendships,
- Learn new perspectives from others, and
- Contribute in meaningful ways to the lives of others.

When we involve our children, they also gain new perspectives, build lasting skills, and strengthen their Character Quality of Service. Being able to contribute to others rather than being self-centered has long-lasting implications:

> "In essence, generativity is the act of preparing another's garden for spring. It's power in the service of love. It's an act of giving that enables another person to manifest his or her own strengths and gifts through love. It can be as simple as listening and giving support to others—renewing their sense of self and hope. It can be as demanding as raising a child well, or mentoring a student in a difficult and challenging field.... [G]enerativity in *high school* predicts good physical and mental health in late adulthood, a time interval of over *fifty* years."[95] Stephen Post

If we feel uncertain about or even resistant to being involved in our community, we can think about this:

> "It may seem as if individuals and families that are struggling to address their own needs in a disintegrating social order have no time for community building. Yet, it is precisely in the context of the community that they will find the means to solve their problems. … When each member of the community seeks to address the well-being of the others, the powers of the community are multiplied and all receive blessings and assistance in a way that attending to one's own problems can never achieve."[96]
> Paul Lample

Some community-building ideas for us to consider are:

- Facilitate a study session or ongoing group to explore a meaningful or interesting topic
- Host a prayer gathering and/or a consultation focused on a community issue
- Visit neighbors and friends in their homes or a neighborhood gathering place
- Coordinate or participate in a community improvement project
- Volunteer our time to support a worthy cause
- Visit or volunteer at an elder care facility or help the elderly in their homes
- Offer classes for the moral and spiritual education of children
- Offer friendship, mentorship, and guidance to groups of pre-teens or teens
- Join a committee addressing a civic or social issue
- Encourage people's participation in the arts
- Volunteer at a museum, concert hall, theater, or library

A Couple Shares Their Experience: *"Over the summer while our children were out of school, we moved to a more diverse neighborhood inside a city and near a park and playground. It was an adjustment to live closer to more people, but we soon discovered how easy it was to have conversations with others. We got involved at a community center where there were activities for children and teens. Soon it became natural for us and the other parents to come together and address our mutual concerns."*

As we expand our couple and family circle to include others, our lives become richer, we find new opportunities to strengthen our Character Qualities, and we lift our eyes from our daily responsibilities. We remember to apply Moderation to ensure our home life is taken care of. Each time we reach out, we learn we are connected to many others who care.

Examples:

- Enjoy a once-a-month social time with friends.
- Organize and host a neighborhood picnic.
- Facilitate a teen group or offer a class for children.
- Foster children.
- Set up a literacy program or tutor a student.
- Host constructive consultations about social issues such as poverty, racism, or the environment.
- Volunteer with a civic, arts, or healthcare organization.
- Participate in an annual food drive for those in need.

Applying Character Qualities:

Below are some practical ways to incorporate character into daily practices with the theme of this chapter.

Friendliness

- Reach out to create and participate in new friendships.
- Spend time with people to build and maintain friendships.
- Establish relationships and spend time with other healthy and supportive couples and families.

Purposefulness

- Create a value or purpose statement that will motivate our long-term engagement with others.
- Survey our connections with our friends, neighbors, and community to determine what to invest time in.
- Assess the needs of neighbors and our community in consultation with others and carry out actions to contribute to improvements.

Respect

- Ensure that community-based plans and actions are consultative and have leaders from among those who will be most affected.
- Interact with others in ways that build positive mutual regard and willing cooperation.
- Contribute to and accompany others in ways that better their lives, elevate their perspective about the community, and inspire them to demonstrate Service to others.

Learning Activities:

1. Identify someone or a couple we want to build or strengthen a friendship with. Consult about how to begin the process, create a specific plan, and carry it out. Reflect afterward on the experience and consult about the next steps.

2. Plan and carry out an occasion that allows us to practice offering hospitality. Determine together what quality of experience we want our guests to have. To practice Unity, we ensure ahead of time that we are clear and agree about our roles and responsibilities. Assess how to manage our energy before, during, and after the activity, so we stay in balance.

3. Participate in a couple's enrichment group with like-minded couples focused on relationship learning and growth.

4. Invite single people who do not have a partner to our home for dinner. Encourage them to ask questions about our relationship and how we assist each other to grow.

5. Study the United Nations Sustainable Development Goals (https://sdgs.un.org/goals). Consult together about how they could apply in our home. Consult with others in our neighborhood or community about which one(s) we could focus on for improvement. Create concrete plans and action steps with accountability to make progress toward the goal(s) we choose.

6. Meet with a small number of neighbors and consult about ways to improve the socio-economic conditions and/or environment in the area. Create concrete plans and action steps with accountability to make progress toward the goal.

Couple Reflection and Consultation:

Throughout this couple guide, there are invitations to practice the Character Quality of Reflection about your interactions and connection. This practice gives you opportunities to celebrate progress and consult to address issues.

1. What perspectives do we have about expanding our circle of unity to include others?
2. How can we begin new friendships? Establish strong and healthy friendships with other couples?
3. What can we do to sustain friendships over time?
4. How do we prepare ourselves and our home for guests? What aspects of offering hospitality make us feel happy? What stresses us instead? How can we manage that response?
5. How does hospitality contribute to our building of friendships?
6. What actions do we consider particularly thoughtful or kindly helpful to a friend? A neighbor?
7. Do we consider ourselves leaders, followers, or both when engaging in community betterment?
8. How can we contribute to creating a flourishing community with our neighbors and friends?
9. What do we see as the needs of our community? Who could we consult with to better understand them? What do we see as our role in addressing the identified needs?
10. Who do we know that we could invite to participate in community building or betterment with us?
11. What community groups or organizations already exist for us to collaborate with?
12. What could we carry out with specific others that would improve their lives, strengthen their ability to be community leaders and contributors, and bring them joy? When would we do direct action? Instead, when would they act while we accompany them with encouragement and consultation?

Reflecting and Consulting on Our Commitments

We have been gaining new knowledge and trying out new actions throughout this guide to couple vitality. It's useful for us to reflect, consult, and write down the elements that work well for us and that encourage us to keep growing our relationship.

These elements are now becoming our commitment statements that guide our specific and consistent actions. We base our commitments on the Core Elements, Character Qualities, and Vitalizers. Each of these commitments then contributes to our unity.

We use these commitments as goals to strive for, and we also give ourselves the mercy and grace to not be perfect in achieving them. Not everything can be accomplished at once. We will have regular opportunities to:

- Use Reflection
- Consult
- Assess our progress
- Refine our commitments
- Set goals for new actions

Couples Share Their Experiences

Below are some additional ideas, advice, and examples from couples that we used for inspiration as we created our commitment statements.

Including Character Qualities

"We recently had our 10th anniversary, so we made a list of 10 Character Qualities that we commit to call on for the next 10 years. They are acceptance, compassion, creativity,

discernment, grace, kindness, prayerfulness, sacrifice, trust, and dependability."

"We commit to practice being courteous, kind, patient, and loving to each other."

"We will use daily verbal appreciation with each other and our children in the form of Character Quality Language™ acknowledgments."

Daily Practices

"We once got advice from an elderly couple who always looked as if they had just fallen in love with each other. Their secret was they never went to sleep at night upset with each other. They also turned toward each other and asked if any words or actions throughout the day had caused hurt feelings. If they had, they would apologize. If this was practiced by all couples, it would probably result in more successful relationships and marriages and a guarantee of a good night's sleep!" [***Note:*** There are times when exhaustion at night makes consulting and resolving issues unwise and this is best left for the next day, so please use discernment and wisdom.]

Raising Children

"Have a family meeting or a couple meeting and negotiate who will do what chores so that there is a fair distribution of work. Start children on chores very young by giving them a list of what needs to be done that they can do and having them pick. Our boys loved this and did it every Saturday before play or any outing. Our younger son at age 3 put a happy face beside his choices, and our older son printed his name. We had a process where they took turns picking, then spent a couple of hours

doing the chores. In a family consultation, they decided they would do the work on Saturdays instead of every day. It worked well!"

Personal and Couple Behavior

"We chose these commitments:

- *Be friends with each other and be united in mind, body, heart, and soul.*
- *Treat others, and especially each other, family, and friends with love, courtesy, and integrity.*
- *Encourage and accompany one another's personal growth and transformation and the transformation of others.*
- *Regularly, lovingly, and tactfully share any hurts or annoyances we feel, using 'I feel…' terms rather than 'You do…' language. Set up a regular time to share openly and honestly.*
- *Demonstrate Respect for our own and each other's physical, mental, emotional, and spiritual needs, and assist each other to meet those needs as much as possible.*
- *Pray together daily.*
- *Respond to issues that arise as quickly as possible, using consultation as a tool in all matters.*
- *Demonstrate and accept affection and intimacy from one another regularly.*
- *Practice Service with each other, our families, friends, and communities.*
- *Be playful, have fun, and incorporate humor into daily life.*
- *Have regular family meetings for consultation, problem-solving, and planning.*

- *Be patient, accepting, and nurturing, maintaining the constancy of our relationship through times of adversity and when we are not being our best selves."*

Musician and vocalist Elika Mahony shared a blog posting about the significant items, in no particular order, that have contributed to the progress of her marriage to her husband Tarry. They are:

- *"Learning about the needs of one another,*
- *Being thoughtful,*
- *Paying attention to and giving priority to our relationship,*
- *Spending quality time together,*
- *Serving and praying together,*
- *Learning how to communicate and consult more effectively,*
- *Reading and studying books together on varying subjects including the subjects of love and marriage,*
- *Learning about each other's love language (read a book called The Five Love Languages),*
- *Having a weekly lunch date to check in with one another and plan (this has been especially effective),*
- *Having a day date occasionally (setting aside time to go for an outing)"*

She added: *"Of course, there are more things on the list, but these are the ones that stood out for us."*[97]

Continuing Learning and Strengthening

"In the early part of our marriage, we discovered that reflecting on our progress every three months kept us in action.

After that, we made reviewing our list of commitments an annual part of celebrating our anniversary.

"We did this annual reflection, we noticed that the same item was unfulfilled two years in a row. That prompted us to consult about whether we were committed to it. When we agreed this item would still be good to have as part of our marriage, we put more reminders and actions into place, and then we made better progress."

Creating Our Commitments

1. Reflect, consult, and determine what unified actions we are committed to carrying out. Write down our commitment statements to guide us in creating vitality in our relationship. We will include key practices from the Core Elements, Character Qualities, and Vitalizers that are most important to us.

2. Create a visible reminder for us of our commitments.

3. Set a regular interval to review our commitments, such as quarterly or annually. Plan a celebration of our accomplishments. Assess this interval, as it may support us to practice Reflection daily, weekly, or monthly instead.

Reviewing Our Process

As we review our learning from throughout this book, we have a greater appreciation for our process of growth. We can see that we have strengthened our ability to reflect, consult, and develop our Character Qualities and the Vitalizers. Our connection and unity have grown. We realize that this is a continuous process, and it's one we welcome. We celebrate our progress!

Note: In the process of your study and practicing the Core Elements, Character Qualities, and Vitalizers, you may have discerned that you have issues to address beyond the scope of this book. We hope you will seek help from other sources, organizations, and professionals as needed. However, most people, no matter what their issues, benefit from sincerely strengthening their Character Qualities, so we hope you will do that in parallel.

The Non-End

This book is for you to use repeatedly over time as your process of growth continues. Referring to this material will assist you to keep developing the Core Elements, Character Qualities, and Couple Vitalizers. With practice, these will become part of the culture of your relationship. You will continually improve the quality of your life together.

Couple Vitality will also accompany you in fulfilling the vision you developed in "Vitalizer 3: Where Are We Going?". It will accompany you as you strive to fulfill the commitments you wrote down in the last section, "Reflecting and Consulting on Our Commitments". Remember to put in place the reminders that will prompt you to reflect, consult, and act to make progress.

You are probably noticing that your experiences as a couple are contributing to your individual character growth. In turn, your individual growth is also contributing to the quality of your couple experiences. Healthy individuals with many character strengths are more capable of creating couple connection and unity.

As you grow more connected and committed as a united couple, you will experience an increase in your vitality. When you are happy as a couple, you will more consistently serve each other, your family, your friends, and your community.

Your commitment to creating a couple relationship filled with character strengths and vitality will spread the light of unity in the world.

Well done! Please keep on going!

Susanne M. Alexander and W. Grant Peirce IV

References

Welcome!

[1] Drs. Les and Leslie Parrott, *Relationships*, p. 11
[2] Kevin Leman, *Have a New Husband by Friday*, p. 27

Section 1: Powerfully Creating Vitality

[3] Raymond and Furugh Switzer, *Mindful Matrimony*, p. 259
[4] Scott M. Stanley, *Power of Commitment*, pp. 23-24
[5] "Hardwired to Connect: The New Scientific Case for Authoritative Communities", Commission on Children at Risk, 2003
[6] Summarized from Dr. Sue Johnson, *Hold Me Tight*, pp. 21-24
[7] Les and Leslie Parrott, David H. Olson, *Helping Couples*, p. 43
[8] Susan Heitler, PhD, *Power of Two*, p. 11
[9] Frank Pittman, quoted in Thomas Lickona, *Character Matters*, p. 4
[10] Blaine Fowers, *Beyond the Myth of Marital Happiness*, p. 115
[11] Harville Hendrix and Helen LaKelly Hunt, *Getting the Love You Want*, 3rd ed., p. 84
[12] John Gottman and Nan Silver, *Seven Principles for Making Marriage Work*, 2nd ed., p. 27

Section 2: Creating Shared Values and Vision

[13] Susan Page, essay in Susanne M. Alexander, *All-in-One Marriage Prep*, pp. 284-285
[14] Stephen M. R. Covey, *The Speed of Trust*, pp. 67-68
[15] Morrie Schwartz, quoted in Mitch Albom, *Tuesdays with Morrie*, p. 149
[16] Patricia Love and Steven Stosny, *How to Improve Your Marriage Without Talking About It*, p. 100; p. 105
[17] Judith S. Wallerstein and Sandra Blakeslee, *Good Marriage*, pp. 68-69
[18] George S. Pransky, *The Relationship Handbook*, pp. 184-185
[19] W. H. Murray, *The Scottish Himalayan Expedition*, pp. 6-7

Section 3: Creating Loving Partnership

[20] John M. Gottman, Ph.D., and Nan Silver, *Seven Principles for Making Marriage Work*, 2nd ed., pp. 21-22; 28

[21] Shaunti Feldhahn, *The Surprising Secrets of Highly Happy Marriages*, pp. 145-147
[22] Patricia Love, *Truth About Love*, pp. 166-167
[23] Hunt Harville Hendrix and Helen LaKelly Hunt, *Getting the Love You Want*, 3rd ed., Preface, p. xx
[24] John M. Gottman and Nan Silver, *Seven Principles for Making Marriage Work*, 2nd ed., p. 54
[25] Summarized from Kathlyn Hendricks and Gay Hendricks, *Conscious Heart*, pp. 267-272
[26] Patty Howell, https://www.yourtango.com/experts/patty-howell/nurturing-yourself-widowhood-3
[27] Marshall B. Rosenberg, *Nonviolent Communication, A Language of Compassion*, 2nd ed., pp. 41-46
[28] Les and Leslie Parrott and David H. Olson, *Helping Couples*, p. 43
[29] Marital Equality: Gender and Power in Couples Therapy, http://www.marriageandfamilyresearchinstitute.com/Marital-Equality.html
[30] Kathlyn Hendricks and Gay Hendricks, *Conscious Heart,* p. 54; p. 31
[31] Mary Beth George, "What Does Trust and Commitment Look Like in a Relationship", https://www.gottman.com/blog/what-does-trust-and-commitment-look-like-in-a-relationship/
[32] Gary Chapman, T*he Five Love Languages*, p. 24
[33] Summarized from Gary Chapman, *The Five Love Languages*, and quoted in Susanne M. Alexander, *Pure Gold: Encouraging Character Qualities in Marriage*, 2nd ed., p. 75
[34] Sandra Gray Bender, *Recreating Marriage with the Same Old Spouse*, pp. 11-12; p. 15
[35] Daniel C. Jordan, "Becoming Your True Self", p. 5
[36] Les and Leslie Parrott and David H. Olson, *Helping Couples*, p. 51
[37] Tara Parker-Pope, *For Better*, pp. 275-276
[38] Paul Coleman, *30 Secrets of Happily Married Couples*, p. 161
[39] Linda Kavelin Popov, *Family Virtues Guide*, p. 250
[40] Richard Carlson and Joseph Bailey, *Slowing Down to the Speed of Life*, p. 121
[41] John Gottman and Nan Silver, *Seven Principles for Making Marriage Work*, 2nd ed., p. 27
[42] Raymond and Furugh Switzer, *Mindful Matrimony*, pp. 127-128
[43] Linda Kavelin Popov, quoted in Susanne M. Alexander, *Pure Gold*, p. 52
[44] Summarized from John Gottman and Nan Silver, *Seven Principles for Making Marriage Work*, 2nd ed., Ch. 3

---

[45] A.C.M.E./Better Marriages, "Creative Use of Conflict", pp. 5-7; www.bettermarriages.org, used with permission
[46] Les and Leslie Parrott, *When Bad Things Happen to Good Marriages*, p. 42
[47] Raymond and Furugh Switzer, *Mindful Matrimony*, pp. 128-129
[48] Shaunti Feldhahn, *Kindness Challenge*, p. 14

Section 4: Creating Connecting Experiences

[49] John Gottman and Nan Silver, *Seven Principles for Making Marriage Work*, 2nd ed., pp. 88-89
[50] Tara Parker-Pope, *For Better*, pp. 271-272
[51] William Doherty, *Take Back Your Marriage*, pp. 130-133
[52] William Doherty, *Take Back Your Marriage*, p. 131
[53] Rob Skuka, "The Values and Rituals of Authentic Relationships: What the Relationship Enhancement Model Teaches Us About Marriage" quoted in Susanne M. Alexander, *All-in-One Marriage Prep*, pp. 282-283
[54] William Doherty, *Take Back Your Marriage*, pp. 130-133
[55] Claudia and David Arp, *10 Great Dates to Energize Your Marriage*, p. 12
[56] Les and Leslie Parrott and David H. Olson, *Helping Couples*, pp. 43-44
[57] Jeanette C. Lauer and Robert H. Lauer, *The Play Solution*, p. 75
[58] Susan Sparks, *Laugh Your Way to Grace—Reclaiming the Spiritual Power of Humor*, pp. 9-10
[59] Stephen Post, *Why Good Things Happen to Good People*, p. 144
[60] Sharon Salzberg, *Loving-Kindness, The Revolutionary Art of Happiness*, p. 119
[61] Susan Sparks, *Laugh Your Way to Grace, Reclaiming the Spiritual Power of Humor*, p. 97
[62] Sandra Gray Bender, *Recreating Marriage with the Same Old Spouse*, p. 131
[63] "Marriage, Increase the Joy, Decrease the Misery: Service, A Key to Unlocking the Door to a Healthy and Happy Marriage", National Healthy Marriage Institute; http://healthymarriagetips.com/service.htm
[64] Willard F. Harley, Jr., *His Needs, Her Needs*, p. 19
[65] Richard Paul Evans, http://m.huffpost.com/us/entry/6958222.html
[66] Howard J. Markman, Scott M. Stanley, and Susan L. Blumberg, *Fighting for Your Marriage*, pp. 276-277
[67] Susanne M. Alexander, "Sharing Expectations and Meeting One Another's Needs"

Section 5: Forging Deeper Connection

[68] https://www.getlasting.com/marriage-advice
[69] Sue Johnson, *Hold Me Tight*, p. 186
[70] Scott Haltzman, *Secrets of Happily Married Women*, pp. 150-151
[71] Sandra Anne Taylor, *Secrets of Attraction*, p. 195
[72] Raymond and Furugh Switzer, *Mindful Matrimony*, p. 157
[73] Michele Weiner Davis, *The Sex-Starved Marriage*, pp. 11-12
[74] Barry and Emily J. McCarthy, *Getting it Right the First Time: Creating a Healthy Marriage*, pp. 78-79
[75] Syble Solomon, "With Money, What's Really Going On?" Essay included in Susanne M. Alexander, *All-in-One Marriage Prep*, p. 377
[76] Natalie H. Jenkins, Scott M. Stanley, William C. Bailey, and Howard J. Markman, *You Paid How Much for That?!*, p. 17
[77] Mehri Sefidvash, *Coral and Pearls*, pp. 27-28
[78] Joan B. Hernández, *Love, Courtship, and Marriage*, p. 28
[79] Les and Leslie Parrott, *When Bad Things Happen to Good Marriages*, p. 120
[80] Les and Leslie Parrott, *When Bad Things Happen to Good Marriages*, p. 132
[81] Stephen Post, *Why Good Things Happen to Good People*, p. 114
[82] Michele Weiner-Davis, *Divorce Busting*, pp. 232-233
[83] Summarized from Gary Chapman and Jennifer Thomas, *When Sorry Isn't Enough*
[84] Les and Leslie Parrott, *When Bad Things Happen to Good Marriages*, p. 142
[85] Stephen Post, *Why Good Things Happen to Good People*, p. 104
[86] Howard J. Markman, Scott M. Stanley, Susan L. Blumberg, Natalie H. Jenkins, and Carol Whiteley, *12 Hours to a Great Marriage*, p. 207

Section 6: Expanding Beyond Us

[87] Janet A. Khan, *Prophet's Daughter*, p. 245
[88] Linda Kavelin Popov, *Family Virtues Guide*, pp. 29-30
[89] Monette Van Lith, *Family Matters*, p. 30
[90] Virginia Satir, *The New Peoplemaking*, Ch. 1
[91] Raymond and Furugh Switzer, *Mindful Matrimony*, p. 256
[92] Stephen R. Covey, *The 7 Habits of Highly Effective Families*, p. 72

---

[93] Agnes Ghaznavi, *Family Repairs and Maintenance Manual*, pp. 41-43
[94] Susan Sparks, *Laugh Your Way to Grace—Reclaiming the Spiritual Power of Humor*, p. 68
[95] Stephen Post, *Why Good Things Happen to Good People*, pp. 47; 49
[96] Paul Lample, *Creating a New Mind*, p. 112

Reflecting on Our Commitments

[97] https://www.elikamahony.com; January 8, 2019

Expressing Our Gratitude

We are grateful to our families, clients, online course participants, and workshop participants who contributed anonymously to this book. We are also grateful to the following people who generously took time to provide input and encouragement:

> Anne Bivans, Paul Blois, Glenn Booth, Raven Deerwater, Rebecca Deerwater, Fanya DeMaria, Phil Donihe, Michelle Farnsworth, Priscilla Hunt, Jane Ives, Paul Kuhn, Pat Love, Rebecca Marshall, Fiona McDonald, Ana Morante, Nisa Muhammad, Jackie Najafian, Patricia O'Connor, Elisabeth Pereira, Guillermo Rein, Syble Solomon, Cecile Wabnitz, Johann Wong, and Johanna Merritt Wu.

Thank you as well to George Ronald, Publisher, for permission to quote from *Mindful Matrimony* and to Better Marriages (www.bettermarriages.org) for permission to quote from their materials.

About the Authors and Our Contact Information

Susanne M. Alexander

Susanne M. Alexander is a Relationship and Marriage Educator and Coach, book author, and publisher with Marriage Transformation®. She is certified to offer couple's assessments through Prepare-Enrich® and for individuals with the Character Foundations Assessment™.

Susanne is passionate about facilitating individuals and couples making good character, relationship, and marriage choices through building knowledge and skills. Couples who make excellent choices create happy, healthy relationships and marriages and prevent divorces. Susanne meets with individual and couple clients globally via the internet for character growth, relationship and marriage preparation, and couple relationship and marriage strengthening.

Susanne writes articles and books about character, relationships, and marriage. She also develops online courses for healthy relationships, marriages, and families. She is a member of the National Alliance for Relationship and Marriage Education (NARME).

Susanne shares: "I have had an adventurous time with relationships and marriages. My first marriage gave me a daughter—and now son-in-law and two granddaughters. However, it was very difficult, as he had many illnesses. The marriage ended in divorce when our daughter was 18. I married again, a very happy marriage, with three young adult stepchildren. We offered marriage preparation and marriage enrichment efforts together. This second husband died from brain cancer just before our 10th wedding anniversary. Matching websites, dating experiences, and moving led me to

---

find a third husband with two adult stepchildren, and we are in a happy marriage.

"With all these adventures, along with professional education, I have had many opportunities to experience, observe, and learn about the importance of finding someone with many character strengths to marry and then building a good marriage partnership with them. It has not been easy, but when I have learned relationship skills and when marriage works well with love, friendship, and consultation, it's a great place to be."

Susanne is originally from Canada and now lives with her husband Phil L. Donihe in Tennessee, in the United States. They often collaborate in working with individuals and couples. He is a coach and also certified with the Character Foundations Assessment™.

Susanne's books can be purchased through her website www.marriagetransformation.com and many other online bookstores. Anyone wishing a discount on bulk purchases for group use or for re-selling should contact her directly.

Susanne M. Alexander
P. O. Box 249, Harrison, TN, 37341-0249, United States
+1 423.599.0153 (US Eastern time zone)
Susanne@marriagetransformation.com
www.marriagetransformation.com
www.transformationlearningcenter.com
https://www.instagram.com/marriagetransformation/
Twitter: marriage4ever
https://www.facebook.com/MarriageTransformation
https://www.linkedin.com/in/susannemalexander/
https://www.youtube.com/user/SusanneMAlexander

W. Grant Peirce IV

W. Grant Peirce IV is an Industrial and Organizational Psychologist with a passion for helping individuals and organizations succeed with integrity and purpose.

Grant serves as the Founder and CEO of Peirce Group Organizational Effectiveness Consultants. Grant is the author of the Character Foundations Assessment™ (CFA), a tool designed to help individuals and organizations develop their fundamental character and make the conscious decisions necessary to achieve true and sustainable success. He is a member of the American Psychological Association, Society for Industrial and Organizational Psychology, and the American Educational Research Association.

Grant's interest in character began with raising his daughters. He says, "At a young age, they were exposed to character education. It was amazing to see how much they connected with the Character Qualities and have used and strengthened them throughout their lives and on into their young adulthood. It's still a big part of how we communicate as a family today."

After seeing the effectiveness of character education in children, Grant began to see the potential for character development in adults. "Because my profession was in organizational development, I first focused on character development for business leaders. While they found developing Character Qualities through the CFA instrumental in leading their organizations, many of my clients also asked me to have their marriage partners take the CFA, so they could use the Character Qualities to help vitalize their marriages."

Grant's interest in character development in couples is also inspired by his marriage. "Our marriage has been an adventure, starting as young graduate students in Chicago, having children, living in China for three years, moving back to Chicago, and then to Boston. We have had some real high points and some challenges, but our focus on the Character Qualities have always kept us grounded."

Couple Vitality is part of Grant's ongoing effort to bring character development to the entirety of people's lives. "Our personal character affects every aspect of our lives and every relationship we have. I love to see the natural joy people receive when they exhibit a character strength or when they can entice it out of others."

Grant and Deborah, his wife of 25 years, have two adult daughters, and they live in Massachusetts in the United States.

W. Grant Peirce IV
224 Old Marlboro Road
Concord, MA, 01742-4128, United States
+1 847.932.9621 (US Eastern time zone)
grantpeirce@peircegroup.com
www.peircegroup.com
www.linkedin.com/in/grantpeirce

CharacterYAQ

Susanne M. Alexander and W. Grant Peirce IV are collaborators on the topic of character in relationships, business, and other aspects of life along with Johann S. Wong in an initiative called CharacterYAQ, www.characteryaq.com.

The Vision for this initiative is: "Creating joyful and sustainable character-based relationships among individuals, couples, families, communities, and workplaces."

We are committed to demonstrating:

- Creativity with Excellence.
- Positive Spirit with love and Friendliness.
- Truthfulness with Reflection and integrity.
- Service with Humility and Compassion.
- Unity with Respect and Justice.
- Respect for all people as noble human beings engaged in personal transformation.
- Purposefulness with meaningful and positive outcomes.

Please see www.characteryaq.com for more information on character and our products and services.

Lightning Source UK Ltd.
Milton Keynes UK
UKHW022010090223
416682UK00013B/1159

9 781940 062297